—overeat?
—perform poorly?
—complain repeatedly about the same problem?
—get depressed?
—get stymied on important projects?
—feel trapped in relationships?
—have chronic problems with supervisors even though you do your job well?

It's time you discovered where your "ostrich" is hiding. *The Ostrich Complex*, an analysis and guide to self-assessment, is designed to help you understand and overcome the fears that stand in your way, become the kind of person you want to be, and achieve your lifelong goals.

❏   ❏   ❏

It will help you develop in yourself the characteristics that can turn you from an earthbound ostrich to an "eagle" that soars to success.

Please turn this page for the professionals' acclaim for *The Ostrich Complex*.

THE OSTRICH

"Most anyone will recognize a bit of the 'ostrich' in him or herself while reading this book. And...will find Elliot Weiner's ways of attacking the old bird very, very helpful."

—**Marjorie Hansen Shaevitz,
Director of the Institute for
Family and Work Relationships,
La Jolla, California, and author
of *The Superwoman Syndrome***

"Dr. Weiner's prescription for freeing ourselves from Ostrich habits is creative, realistic and immensely workable. Best of all, he's offering techniques that make the 'doing' as enjoyable as the results."

—**Joy Davidson, Ph.D.,
Human Behavior Columnist,
*Los Angeles Times Syndicate***

"Sure to appeal to anyone who hesitates before decision-making."

—*Library Journal*

COMPLEX

"Pull out your heads, shake off the sand, and open your minds. Elliot Weiner writes just to you. He gives you permission to be guilty of the ostrich complex. He even admits to its affliction himself. *The Ostrich Complex* is a warm, personal and personable prescription for going beyond those fears that have held you back for far too long. It's a book written with *you* in mind, in a wonderful style that says, 'We can lick this together.' Hang on and follow Elliot step-by-step. He'll lead you on your way. You won't even realize that you're doing most of the work yourself. Waste no more time. Stretch to your limits, flutter your wings and move on. Life is flying by."

—Robin Lawson, President,
Enrichment Unlimited,
Portland, Oregon

THE OSTRICH COMPLEX

A PERSONALIZED PLAN OF ACTION FOR OVERCOMING THE FEARS THAT HOLD YOU BACK

ELLIOT WEINER, Ph.D.

WARNER BOOKS

A Warner Communications Company

The Ostrich Complex is based upon an original concept and title by M. J. Abadie.

WARNER BOOKS EDITION

Cover design by Anthony Russo

Warner Books, Inc.
666 Fifth Avenue
New York, N.Y. 10103

 A Warner Communications Company

Printed in the United States of America

This book was originally published in hardcover by Warner Books.
First Printed in Paperback: February, 1987

10 9 8 7 6 5 4 3 2 1

For Natalie and Neal
May the sand be always beneath your feet

Acknowledgments

No ostrich, not even a reformed one, can write a book alone, so this project was truly a collaborative effort. I want to thank the talented and kind people who have been with me during my writing of this book. Little would be on these pages if it were not for them.

My first and foremost thanks go to my agent, Sherry Robb, a creative and sensitive friend; and to my supportive and insightful editor and vice-president at Warner Books, Fredda Isaacson. This project would not have been completed, let alone started, without them. Their ideas and spirit helped bring this concept alive. Whatever kind words you may have after using this book should be shared equally with them.

My gifted colleagues, George Csicsery, M.S., and Richard Brzustowicz, M.S., gave willingly of their ideas and energies to help make this book what it is, and I thank them for all that they have done.

Thanks to Bernard Shir-Cliff, editor-in-chief at Warner Books, who with Fredda, Sherry, and me over breakfast in Washington, D.C., helped find the direction this project should take. And thanks to Larry Kirshbaum, president, and all of the other talented and enthusiastic people at Warner Books, who welcomed me with open arms and are helping my ideas make it beyond these pages.

Thank you, Larry, for your initial trust; Rita, for your energies, friendship, and tender caretaking of my career; and you, Barbara, for always believing, and helping me to believe, that I really can write.

Thank you, Suz, for your loving support and creative ideas.

Thank you, Susan, for your caring, friendship, and love.

Thank you, Natalie and Neal—what great people you are! I love you for who you are and for all that you continue to give me.

Sincere appreciation to Bart Andrews and Stephanie Rick and all my other friends, students, and clients, corporate and individual, who've worked with me over the years to help me develop an awareness and understanding of the Ostrich Complex, and to my colleagues whose ideas and research into related concepts have served as the background for my own.

Thanks to my Macintosh. I couldn't have done it without you.

And thanks with apologies to all the ostriches in the wilds and in the zoos. I know that you really just lay your head along the ground and don't bury it in the sand. Thanks for lending me this metaphor.

Contents

os·trich com·plex, the (äs′ trich käm′ pleks, the)
noun. Origin: American 1. the state or condition of ignoring, avoiding, or pretending that
something doesn't exist with the hope that the
something, usually a problem, will just go
away 2. the tendency to defer small problems
until they become large ones 3. a psychological
term sometimes referred to as the *head-in-the-
sand syndrome* 4. a habit used in times or
conditions of personal stress and/or anxiety 5. a
defense mechanism usually implemented to cover up a deep fear of loss, anger, insecurity, or
loss of self-esteem 6. an apparently benign
condition which, if left untreated, can become
a major corporate and personal malady

Prologue

Your Hunt Begins

The ostrich believes she is hidden from view
with her foolish head stuck in the ground.
For she thinks you can't see her when she
can't see you,
So the ostrich is easily found.

This is one of my children's favorite poems. Now it is one of mine, because I found that I was that ostrich.

I am now on the road to being reformed. What about you?

- Do you avoid confrontations because you fear the other person may not love you if you disagree?
- Do you find yourself putting a small task off until tomorrow . . . and tomorrow . . . and tomorrow—only to find that it has become a major obstacle by the time you tackle it?
- Do you find it difficult to forgive and forget, storing up things that bother you rather than dealing with them as you would like to?

- Do you often find yourself at work piling up memos and telephone calls that need to be answered because you "just can't find the time" to handle each one as it comes up?
- Do you feel compelled to do even small jobs "just right" or refuse to attempt them at all—until they become huge, emotionally draining final tasks?

If you have answered yes to any of these questions, you have a lot of company. These situations—and these reactions—are traps for all of us at one time or another. When faced with unpleasant, stressful demands, we often find ourselves burying our heads alongside the ostrich.

Now you may say, "But I only answered yes to one or two of these questions, so it's not a big problem for me." Think about how even one of these situations, however, can have a far greater negative impact on your life than it should. I'm talking about the pain that accumulates as over and over you avoid dealing with the same situation or the anxiety that comes with a fear of losing someone or something that means a lot to you and which grows as that fear goes unexamined.

If you responded like the proverbial ostrich in any of these situations, your personal or work life may now be filled with major, emotionally draining hurdles. When you first considered the confrontation, the telephone call, or the simple task, it was small and easily managed. When you put it off, or refused to pay attention to it, you no doubt hoped the problem would just go away. But did it?

You and I know what happened to your problem. It got bigger—and bigger. And, as it grew, it started demanding more and more of your emotional energy. It began to weigh you down.

I know that's been true for me. Before I began to develop my own understanding of the Ostrich Complex, I often found myself sitting in my office or lying in bed trying *not* to think about the unpleasant tasks that I had to do. These were problems such as dealing with a client who hadn't paid a bill, or calling the tenants in our rental duplex about a problem in their care of the property, or discussing with a loved one a problem that had come up between us, or . . . My list went on and on.

I found myself thinking one or more of the following: "Well, I really don't have the time to do it as well as it needs to be done, so I'll wait" (perfectionism); or, "I'll take care of these other things today and then get to that problem" (procrastination); or, "Well, my relationship with Lynn really isn't all that bad so why make it worse by talking about problems?" (denial); or, "I'm concerned about Mike's reactions to what I need to tell him, so I'll give him a few more chances" (collecting).

Whatever the symptom of my head-in-the-sand behavior, the result was the same: A small problem got much bigger. One of the main points that I want you to learn from my experience is that it doesn't have to happen that way.

I hope it will stop happening that way for you. That's why I've written—and you're reading—this book.

The Ostrich Complex is a common condition. You and I have had a lot of ostriching company over the years. Nero was not alone when he put off calling in the Roman bucket brigade until he was done fiddling his tune; the Roman writer Pliny the Elder described many of his other countrymen as ostriches, "the veriest fools they be of all others, for as high as the rest of their body is, yet if they thrust their head and neck once into any shrub or bush, and get it hidden, they think then they are safe enough, and that no man seeth them."

When applied to me or to you—or to major companies with whom I've worked—those words describe what I characterize as the Ostrich Complex. Stemming from worry and fear, and insidiously developed into a habit, this complex guides our thoughts and many of our actions. It keeps us dealing with life in a phony way that prevents us from confronting how we really feel, what we actually want, and what we genuinely deserve. Despite all the times our ostriching hasn't worked, we keep hoping that this time our problems will disappear.

But they don't. They get worse.

In my professional practice I've seen how destructive the Ostrich Complex can be to relationships at work and in love. We'll be discussing many of the people who, through their experiences, have helped me identify the presence of the ostrich in his many guises. You'll meet Glenn and his company, who found that a lack of clear job descriptions and good employer–employee communications allowed a single misunderstanding to develop into a major—and profit-reducing—problem. Later you'll meet Gail, a former client who was so self-deceived by her own ostriching that she could honestly say when her husband "suddenly" announced that he wanted a divorce, "I had no warning."

The ideas in this book reflect what I've learned from many companies about the severe emotional and financial effects that can be attributed to the Ostrich Complex. They reflect what I've learned from my eighteen years of working with individual clients who have permitted initially small problems to grow into major personal maladies. They have developed as well from what I have learned—and am still learning—from dealing with my own Ostrich Complex. Through examples I want to help you spot the dangers in letting small problems go unresolved. In these stories you'll be able to identify the patterns that are relevant to your own work and personal life, and with the techniques I suggest you'll be able to banish the Ostrich Complex so that it no longer inhibits your success and happiness.

PART ONE

Understanding the Ostrich Complex

Chapter 1

The Ostrich Complex Defined

DEIRDRE

Deirdre has just been hired by the law firm she always wanted to work for. She passed the state bar exam in the top 5 percent and got the job because she was highly recommended for her work while she was a legal aide. Although she has yet to prove herself, everyone at the law office considers Deirdre to be "brilliant" and "highly promising." The wind is definitely at her back.

Deirdre, however, has been unable to complete her work on the first two relatively easy cases to which she's been assigned. She has pored over the evidence and has collected precedents for a dozen different arguments, but when it is time to put her conclusions down on paper and submit them to the junior partner assigned to the case, she becomes distracted, unable to function, and filled with panic.

Deirdre has felt this way for two weeks. After another few days her lack of progress is bound to be noticed. She's spoken to some friends outside the legal profession about her problem, but they haven't been able to help. They just tell her to get to work and get the job done. What bothers her most is probably the fact that the present cases are far less complex than the ones she handled as a legal aide. She's started feeling trapped in her office, afraid to walk through the hallways, lest someone ask her how the cases are coming.

Deirdre has no explanation for what's going on, just a feeling of having lost control—for no good reason. Now she's worried that she can't handle the pressure and is thinking about abandoning the legal profession for something easier; but she can't even decide to do that, so she has stuck her head in the sand. It's not that she isn't aware that she has a problem. It's more that she is too afraid to deal with it directly, to examine whatever fear is restricting her abilities, and to face the problem head-on. Her friends have tried to be helpful by telling her that she's too much of a perfectionist, reminding her that she's always been that way, even with men.

Such words don't help. They only add to her feelings of stress, causing her to bury her head more deeply in the sand. We know that if she doesn't pull her head out soon, Deirdre is likely to be abandoned by the legal profession before she can decide whether or not to abandon it herself. Immobilized, she is assuming a posture that can only lead to disaster.

GLENN

On Tuesday afternoon, Glenn returned from lunch to find a note from Sandy, his boss's secretary, stuck to his phone, *"Mr. Stevens wants you in his office ASAP!"*

The reorganization plan Glenn had been assigned wasn't due for another week. The speech he was preparing for the upcoming convention was due for Stevens' review even later. Glenn had no idea why Stevens wanted to see him. As he rode the four floors in the elevator, he shrugged his shoulders, buttoned then unbuttoned his jacket, and gnawed his fingernails.

Sandy greeted him with a nod toward Stevens' office, remaining all the while as inscrutable as a rock.

When Glenn walked into the room, Stevens stood up and folded his arms across his chest. "Well, Glenn," he said, "it's about time. I called you in here to review the accounts you've been switching to the new billing system. I got a call from the head office asking when we'd be finished. I told them that *you* were probably through with them by now."

Glenn froze. The sudden barrage immobilized him. Stevens had never before mentioned switching any accounts to the new billing system—*never.* Glenn wasn't sure that the new system was even operational. But this was no time to panic, even if he felt that Stevens had ambushed him.

Glenn tried to clear his throat—unsuccessfully. In complete disbelief, he heard himself say, "Oh, yes, Mr. Stevens, oh, the accounts. Yes, of course, they're almost ready. They're just taking me longer than I thought they would.'' At the same time his mind kept protesting, *"How can they be ready? I didn't even know about them!"*

What Glenn really wanted to tell Stevens was that he had never been told to switch the accounts, that the delay wasn't his fault, and that he didn't know if the new system was even ready to use.

Instead, Glenn found himself in a dilemma familiar to many of us: He felt he couldn't win no matter what he said or did. No reasonable person would tell Glenn to confront his boss there on the spot. A power play with a boss rarely provides anything except a catharsis—and a brief one at that. As invisible spectators, we would like to see Glenn convey to Stevens that there had been a mix-up and that if he and Stevens could work together on this, both would come out of it in decent shape. But Glenn has a low view of his own abilities and a corresponding negative self-esteem. He has too easily talked himself into believing that all this probably *is* his fault in some way, that he is incompetent and unreliable, and that he was lucky Stevens hadn't fired him there on the spot. He put himself down instead of taking a realistic view of where the fault lay. He chose *not* to convey to Stevens that he felt there had been a misunderstanding and that he was being unfairly accused of inefficiency.

An additional important part of the bind for Glenn was that he had always wanted Stevens to like *him* as well as his work. Now, he found himself afraid that Stevens might be too angry at him to give him another chance. His own self-esteem took a second place to his need to be liked and his fear of being rejected.

You may look at what Glenn did in response to Mr.

Stevens and just shake your head in pity. But ask youself, honestly now, has anything similar ever happened to you? Have you ever responded in a similar way?

Haven't we all played the role of patsy on occasion when we should have spoken up and pointed out that we were being emotionally abused? Haven't all of us pretended that something unpleasant just didn't exist? I know I have buried my head in the sand with some "It'll just go away" hopes. Haven't you?

If you're sure that what happened to Glenn on that Tuesday or Deirdre's ongoing problems just aren't things that could ever happen to you, perhaps you can see yourself in one of the following situations.

MARGARET

Margaret and Craig were hired by the same company at approximately the same time. Through a trusted friend, Margaret learned that her responsibilities were essentially the same as Craig's but that her salary was 18 percent lower. Of course, she's thought about discussing it with her boss. She's even made an appointment, several appointments, actually, but whenever Margaret sees her boss, she experiences such high anxiety that she just mumbles a sentence or two about something else and walks away. She is so afraid he will say she just can't handle the job and the pressure that she can't bring herself to assert her demands. Margaret is so afraid he will confirm her own hidden fears of inadequacy that she prefers to snuggle in that nice warm sand rather than face what *might* be cold truth.

WALTER

Walter has been with the same insurance company for fourteen years. During that time he has carved for himself what he thought was a safe and confortable niche: good raises; just the right amount of responsibility; enough pats on the back from his superiors. In short, Walter has what anyone would call a secure job with a rosy future. Recently, however, his boss hired an attractive woman fresh out of college to work as Walter's assistant. Since he began teaching Jessica much of what he knows about his own job, he has also become fearful that he could be training her as his own replacement.

Walter's new concern has led to a great deal of physical discomfort for him. He has found it difficult to sleep; his appetite has declined; and the quality of his work has slowly deteriorated to a dangerously low level. At home, his wife has warned Walter that if he keeps her awake one more night, he'd better plan on sleeping in the living room.

Yet Walter has refused to discuss with anyone his concerns about why he has been assigned to train Jessica, including his own boss and his wife. When she asks what's wrong, Walter answers, "Things will just work themselves out."

It's obvious that if Walter keeps going in his present direction, he's going to find himself in a tailspin from which it could be almost impossible to recover. The continued deterioration of his performance at work will be noticed, and like a self-fulfilling prophecy, Walter will be replaced in the job he created over fourteen years earlier.

ROY

Roy has been dating Shirley for two years. Recently, he has made all the moves needed to let her know he is interested in what he calls a serious monogamous relationship, even marriage, if Shirley will have him. While Shirley has welcomed Roy's lavish attention, she is always vague about the future. She is most enthusiastic when Roy shows up with an expensive present or takes her out for an exciting evening on the town.

After these two years, Roy tells his friends that he still has no real idea whether Shirley even likes him. Not too long ago, after dinner at the Yuen Gardens, Roy proposed—in a way. The conversation went something like this:

"Shirley, I've been waiting to say this all night."

"Oh, Roy, this dessert is simply fantastic!"

"I'm serious, honey, we have to talk."

"What for? It just ruins everything. What's the matter? Aren't you having fun? I am. Lots."

"Listen, I mean about us—"

"What about us? . . . Oh, look at that guy over there. Isn't it sweet the way he helped her on with her coat. He's really a hunk."

Roy takes a quick look and turns back to Shirley, determined to get her attention. "Shirley, don't you think we've been going together long enough?"

"God, he's gorgeous. What, Roy?"

"Come on, Shirley, I'm serious. Don't you think we've been going together long enough—long enough to make a serious commitment?"

Shirley responds with laughter. "Come on, Roy. You

always want to get serious when we're having fun. Why can't you just loosen up? We'll talk about it some other time."

Roy decides that he can at least find out when *that* time will be. "How about tomorrow? It's Saturday. We can take a picnic lunch and spend the day together talking about us."

Shirley crinkles her nose. "Oh, Roy, I'd love to. But I promised Sally I'd spend the weekend with her helping her figure out how to handle the problems she and Jim are having. You know, they are *really* screwed up. I mean, that girl needs help or she might . . ."

Shirley reaches across the table, touching Roy's hand to show him how much she appreciates his understanding and that she is pleased he hasn't let their far lighter problems get in the way of her need to help a friend.

Sally's name comes up often when Roy wants to spend time with Shirley. Although he suspects once in a while that he's being brushed off, he's never mentioned his suspicions or fears to Shirley. After all, he loves her, and it isn't right to pressure someone you love. Instead of telling her how disappointed he is in her plans to spend the weekend helping Sally with her problems, Roy supports Shirley's decision without a single note of complaint.

Their conversation, as you can imagine, continued along the same established, but unexamined, ground rules, with Roy responding as though everything were all right. The fact is that his feelings during the conversation got more and more confused, but he can't express his frustration to Shirley. He stays afraid that if he does, Shirley may get offended and do something rash.

Now what is the rash behavior that has Roy so frightened? What could Shirley do? She could act annoyed, or even get angry, but she seems to scowl most of the time already. Might she break up with him? Yes, Roy is certainly afraid of that. His fear is that their relationship is so fragile that if he rocks the boat just a little bit, she will use it as an excuse to break up. He's obviously ignoring the fact that their boat is already so full of holes that it is sinking straight to the bottom.

Roy is practicing classic ostrich behavior in his relationship with Shirley. He keeps hoping that everything will work out if he ignores the problems in their relationship. He avoids the symptoms of their difficulties as he would quills on a porcupine. Rather than prick his fingers he looks past the spines. If he doesn't notice them soon, however, he's going to carry his self-esteem straight into even more pain.

THE EFFECTS OF OSTRICHING

Each of these cases shows someone dealing with a problem, task, or critical situation by sticking his or her head in the sand. In each case, and for individual reasons, the person has chosen not to deal directly with the anxiety-producing situation. Each of these cases is a little extreme and is guaranteed to lead to an unpleasant resolution if some direct steps aren't taken. If each of these ostrich behaviors persists, the head-hider will be the one to suffer the consequences—and in most cases, will never realize that he or she has brought the suffering on by his or her *lack* of action.

Let's take a quick look at each of our new friends and

summarize what each problem is and where the ostrich behavior may lead.

Deirdre. Deirdre must take some action immediately or she will be unable to keep her job and her bright future as a lawyer. She must examine the purpose served by her ostrich behavior and deal directly with those fears.

Glenn. If Glenn continues to put himself down and assume that work problems are basically his fault, he will be miserable as long as he stays with that company—and probably with any other company as well. He will become less happy about himself and less efficient in his work; his boss will become more and more demanding; and the company—including Glenn and Mr. Stevens—will suffer the results: compounded effects of poorly defined jobs, resentment of a superior, a negative view of the staff, and poor communication among employees.

Margaret. Margaret's situation is similar. If she does not soon find out why she is getting less money for the same work, she will become even more confused, resentful, and unhappy in her work. Both she and the company will be losers.

Walter. Walter is in a similar dilemma. He must find out if Jessica is going to be his replacement, and, if so, why. If he can face the situation, he may be able to halt the process he fears most, that of training Jessica to be his own replacement. At the very least, Walter can find out why management might be planning to replace him and take steps to deal with the problem—or begin to make other plans. At best, he can use his ability as a mentor as evidence that he is worthy of a higher position. The reality of the situation is probably nowhere near as bad as Walter's imaginary view of it; facing his fears will free him to look for advantages and alternative strategies.

Roy. Roy has little to lose by pulling his head from the sand. Yet he stands to gain respect—from Shirley, and from himself. His ostrich behavior will make it difficult for him ever to move into the mutually satisfying relationship that he seeks.

RECOGNIZING THE OSTRICH COMPLEX

If the Ostrich Complex can wreak so much havoc at the workplace and at home, isn't it a good idea to watch out for it? After all, forewarned is forearmed. If we can train ourselves to watch for the ostrich, then it just might be possible to intervene on our own behalf before our heads get stuck in the sand to the point where we can't pull them out. The question then becomes: How do we recognize the Ostrich Complex so that we can take the proper counter-measures?

Because the Ostrich Complex is so subtle in the way it develops and works, recognizing it is no simple trick. Since ostrich behavior is itself a way of tricking ourselves into *not seeing* something threatening, it makes sense that it is difficult to see from what problem our ostrich side is trying to hide, and, at the same time, protect us. But it can be done. We start by not forcing our ostrich from the sand but, rather, by looking at ostrich behavior as it occurs in others.

In fact, the Ostrich Complex is one of the basic reasons we often find it easier to see faults in others than in ourselves, simpler to analyze the mistakes of others than our own, more effective to assist in correcting the problems of others than to straighten out our own. But what should we look for when trying to uncover ostrich behavior in others? The answer is really very simple: Single out a behavior in someone that you cannot understand or that you find confusing. That problem is very likely to be part of that person's Ostrich Complex.

Confused by a Friend? If another person behaves in a way that makes no sense to you, view that in light of the Ostrich Complex. A friend who makes too many trips to the grocery store in one day, or an office worker who may call you several times a day to discuss trivial points on a joint project, or a child who is constantly behind in his homework even though it's not difficult, or a couple who are always "making up" without ever examining the issues behind their arguments may be offering you clues that something is causing them to hide their heads in the sand. If your own behavior is like this, you might not even be aware of it, but when you have the perspective of a disinterested observer, you can see that a problem exists.

Annoyed? Behavior that you find annoying in others can often be manifestations of the Ostrich Complex, especially when it occurs in people on whom you may occasionally place demands. Take Bob, for example, who owes you some money, which he's agreed to pay back on the fifteenth. Although you usually talk to Bob on the average of three times each week, it is now the twenty-seventh and you have not heard a peep from him since the twelfth. Unless he's contracted a case of total paralysis, it's a good bet that he's not calling because he doesn't want to deal with you and the money he owes you. Bob may not have the money, or he may not be ready to pay you back; but that isn't what you are being told by his ostrich behavior.

Bob is avoiding the issue, or at least trying to, so you don't know what the real reason is he's not paying you. Does he really not have the money? Or is he trying to avoid paying you back—forever? Before you assume the former, that Bob is a deadbeat, think about whether he might just be ostriching. He could choose to be direct and tell you that he just doesn't have the money yet, but that's an uncomfortable thing to do. So he delays telling you, hoping that he won't have to. The longer he waits to call, however, the harder it becomes for him to fess up to you that he's not paying the money on time. He may be saying to himself, "I'll just wait until tomorrow, and then I'll be able to tell him when I can pay him"—and then tomorrow, and tomorrow, and . . .

Words, Words, and More Words. Watch for signs of ostrich behavior in others in their words, as well. People often say more than they realize they are saying, particularly when they complain, so listen to your friends' complaints and worries. Their conversation acts as a lens through which you can view the inner workings of their ostrich.

For example, if your friend Gail takes you to lunch and

confides that she believes her husband is sleeping with another woman, one simple question will tell you whether Gail is playing the ostrich or not: "Have you talked to your husband about this, Gail?" If the answer is no, you can guess that Gail spends a lot of time and effort forcing her head deeper into the sand where her relationship with her husband is concerned.

Simply by confiding in you, Gail is exercising one of the ostrich's favorite behavior patterns: complaining to the wrong person. Actually you're the perfect person for the ostrich. Telling you won't force her to confront the problem and yet may get her sympathy for how tough her life is. You most likely can't—or won't—do anything about what her husband is doing. That makes you that ostrich's favorite air vent. You provide enough air so that she won't suffocate with her head under the sand but still allow her to keep her head buried. The basic idea here in recognizing the Ostrich Complex is that people with ostrich problems express their frustrations, problems, and pain to others, but not to anyone who can help them deal with them directly.

Stress, Stress, and More Stress. When looking for signs of the ostrich in others, look for signs of reaction to stress in their lives. Such signs are usually easy to spot: overeating, poor performance, repeated complaining about the same problem, depression, lack of progress in a work effort or project, signs of being trapped in an oppressive relationship, chronic problems with supervisors despite good performance, and other indications of perennial victimhood are all signs that should be investigated. There may very well be an ostrich lurking behind each one, its head deep in the sand.

After a short time, and a little practice, you will become expert at detecting and analyzing ostrich behavior in others. You will see that the Ostrich Complex is everywhere, and that it exists in milder and more serious variants in almost every person you meet. You will also notice that it is usually the product of stress, anxiety, or fear, whether in someone's personal life or at work. All of us show some ostrich behavior when we encounter a stressful or painful situation that we believe we can't manage effectively through some other approach. Ostrich behavior is often our response to threat—real or imagined.

The ostrich style we use in a particular situation can be quite original and creative. Yet the end result is the same: All ostriches have their heads in the sand. So, creative or typical, original or ordinary, different types of ostrich behavior lead to the same end. And, as you'll see in the next chapter, that end is really part of a vicious cycle that feeds on itself and is difficult to stop, although it can be overcome.

When we take a look at that cycle, we're going to be confronting things that are scary to most of us, which is why the ostrich thrives. But it's information you need to know, and really do want to know. Stick with me and we'll look at the ostrich rules—and the exceptions. We'll examine when ostriching is appropriate and when it's trouble. For now, let's look at our ostrich responses to *danger*.

LOOK OUT! HERE COMES DANGER

Since the Ostrich Complex is a common response to danger, we need to go a bit further than we have and delineate the most common sources of danger in our lives and why the Ostrich Complex is such an easy pattern to use as our defense.

The biggest threats that each of us faces are posed by situations, events, people, or other phenomena that are in fact life-threatening in an immediate way. The possibility of death by accident, disease, war, or violence is a very real, and to some, a constant threat. But what do most of us do about such threats? We go through our day-to-day lives with some recognition of the dangers, but we still try to avoid situations that increase our risk.

For example, we don't knowingly get into cars that have poor brakes; we try to remember to lock our doors and windows before leaving the house or going to sleep; we even carry umbrellas when it looks like rain. These are sensible behaviors. No explanation is needed for why we behave like this.

Then what kind of threats do we meet with ostrich behavior? They are the minor crises of everyday life that occur at work, at home, with people we know, with the things we do. Such crises are rarely life-threatening, but they are often very stressful. If not dealt with well, they can be as dangerous as a loose cannon rolling back and forth on a ship's deck during a storm.

AND HERE COMES STRESS!

The sources of stress have been studied by psychologists and physicians for many years. I know that I meet it daily, both personally and professionally. I make sure that even the corporations with whom I consult understand the significance of stress in their overall picture, and how it affects their people and their profits.

The four causes of stress in the workplace[1] that I most often discuss with my corporate clients are similar to the ones that individuals report to me each day about their home and interpersonal situations. Let's look at these four in terms of your own life.

Too Little Time; Too Much Work. Isn't this one of your major complaints—every day? In my professional practice I frequently hear, "If only I had more time"; "If only I didn't have so much to do, then I could relax"; "How can my wife (husband) expect me to get it done by then? Doesn't she (he) know all the other things I have to do?" Procrastinators, for example, use these catch phrases to excuse their lack of accomplishments. All of us find it stressful when we try to meet other people's expectations as well as our own within set periods of time, but only the ostrich sees the excuses as a way to avoid doing what must be done.

If Only I Didn't Have to Do . . . One of the most frustrating aspects of life is that we often feel we have to do things that we don't really want to do, yet we do them anyway—and probably get angry. There is an ostrich waiting for us along with that anger if we blame others for "making" us do these things. That ostrich is a convenient way to avoid looking at our part in making the decision to do what we really don't want to do. It feels safer to accept an assignment or do a favor than to say, "No, I don't choose to do that," but the result of those buried feelings may produce anxiety, frustration, and stress in us. Adopting this ostrich behavior creates an illusion of safety but may cause a harmful build-up inside us.

Things Just Don't Feel Right. The complaint that things just don't *feel* right usually comes from a refusal to examine what is going on in a situation and decide how to correct it. It's a signal that the ostrich is present, although expectations are unspoken and resentments are buried. We need to pay attention to those feelings and not be afraid of them. They are often the best indicators we have about what really is going on. I ask my clients to put aside pro and con lists when making a decision and concentrate, instead, on what their *feelings* say about the problem.

Why Didn't You Tell Me? One of the basic psychological principles that applies universally is that at work or at home, with animals and people, in order to get others to change their problem behavior or to continue their positive behavior, you must give them feedback. How else can we keep others confident that they are doing what we want of them? As social animals, people respond when they are praised.

From Margaret and Walter who didn't know where they stood in their companies to the spouse who fixes wonderful meals after a day of working and taking care of the children, to the other spouse who regularly pays the bills or fixes the leaks after a stressful day at work, to the child who cleans his room or brings home the A from school— all of us *want and need* feedback from those around us. We need feedback that says, "Good job"; that says, "I acknowledge what you have done (or haven't done)"; that says, "I care enough about you to tell you how I feel." In my clinical work I teach parents that for every criticism they should pass out ten praises. Successful management people have said the same thing for years.

I know that you can see yourself somewhere in these or the earlier examples, and that you have probably personally experienced some of these causes of stress, either at work, at home, or in both situations. We'll talk in a short while about where, specifically, the ostrich lives in your life. For now, let's agree that each of these stress-producing situations can be a trigger for an ostrich reaction. And let's agree that at times the ostrich behavior is both normal and effective—short-term—as you'll see in the next chapter. But there are hidden costs, often very high costs, in behaving like an ostrich.

THE HIDDEN OSTRICH BEHIND THE HIDDEN THREAT

Although ostrich behavior is triggered by a stressful situation, that stress often manifests itself as something else. Psychologists have established that all species respond to threat with a "fight-flight" reaction. We try to ward off threats either by becoming menacing in our own right (fight) or by running away from them (flight). The ostrich's type of flight response, burying one's head in the face of a real (or imagined) threat, is not an effective way to run. One's flanks remain even more vulnerable than before.

Anger—Good and Bad. Many respond to threat with anger. When channeled in an appropriate direction, anger can be an effective way of dealing with stress. When used to cover up a problem and *not* deal with it, however, anger becomes completely ineffective, sometimes even damaging. When flood waters are rising to where you stand, it's fine to blame the river. But you can't *just* blame the river and hope things will change for the better; you've got to move to higher ground. This is the *ineffective* way that the ostrich responds to "Why didn't you tell me?" situations that we discussed earlier.

When we are angry at ourselves, or at something we've done—or wish we'd done—we often look for someone else to blame. It's a "bad day at work; blame the spouse; spouse blames the kids; kids blame the dog" model of life. For the moment, passing the burden of guilt along may release built-up pressure; it may actually seem to be solving a problem—but it's not. It is simply a way of avoiding the responsibility of looking at what really is going on, a way of burying our heads—of copping out, as my children put it.

Loss—Real or Imagined. One of the most common situations that triggers the ostrich complex arises from some loss or threat of loss. In the cases I described earlier, Walter is afraid of losing his job; Margaret is afraid of losing status in her own eyes; Roy is afraid of losing the small amount of affection Shirley now gives him.

Walter's job may indeed be in jeopardy—but, then again, it may not. By burying his head as a response, Walter will never find out which is reality and which is his fantasy. He will probably refuse to deal with the problem until he is actually fired. Then he can take little comfort in being able to say, "See! I knew they were going to fire me!'' Wouldn't it be better for Walter if he found out now what the company had in mind for him, so that he might plan some strategy for dealing with what was really happening? What Walter risks is a short-term anxiety and a possible emotional blow to his ego. Even if his worst fears are borne out, knowing and being able to prepare for losing his job would give him greater long-term gains. Think about how you would like to see Walter handle this situation, remembering that it's easier to see the Ostrich Complex in others than in ourselves.

Loss and Insecurity. Roy is also afraid of loss, and his fears cut to the very essence of his security and self-esteem. He's afraid of losing Shirley. We can guess that deep inside Roy knows how Shirley feels and that she is taking advantage of his unwillingness to take a strong position in their relationship. The fact is, though, it's hard for others to love and respect us when we don't love and respect ourselves. Instead of being true to himself and confronting Shirley with his concerns and suspicions, maybe even getting out of the relationship and going on to a better one with someone else, Roy is burying his head, worrying that he will lose Shirley—an imagined loss, since we know she is not really there.

In both cases, the possibility of loss has triggered a form of ostrich behavior that is quite harmful to each person. The pain in ostrich situations is often intense, the suffering often intense, but so many of us are willing to suffer more over the long term than to deal with a sharp blow now and then to get on the road to recovery. That's the paradox of the Ostrich Complex.

I suspect that all of us have behaved like Walter or Roy (or Glenn, Deirdre, or Margaret) at some time in our lives. Perhaps you are in a situation where you are behaving like one of them right now. And you may be asking how it is possible to behave another way, or even if anyone can behave in another way.

The Ostrich-Free Club. There *are* people who take action immediately or as soon as it's appropriate; people who nearly always seem to know what to do, when to do it—and then do it. If they find themselves ostriching, they let very little pain accumulate before they recognize what they are doing and deal with it.

Such people solve problems when everyone else is still figuring out what the problems are. They get to the top first, and seem to stay there. They are the successful people all of us have tried to emulate at one time or another in business, sports, science, or love. They are the doers, not the talkers. They succeed when the rest of us are still a bit muddled, trying to figure out what is going on. Why? Because they have come to understand that the Ostrich Complex prevents more people from achieving their goals than any real or imagined, physical or psychological problem.

Whether or not they recognize the complex by name, they recognize its presence although it hides behind a number of other forms of behavior. They have made the connection and have taken steps to overcome their own tendency toward ostrich behavior. Each has recognized, as you will, too, that ostriching can become an automatic reaction to almost anything that threatens us and can ruin our lives.

You, too, will come to recognize these behavior patterns in the next chapters and discover your own ostrich style. You will have plenty of opportunity to see where the ostrich patterns of *perfectionism, denial, collecting,* and *procrastination* fit into your own life.

This analysis and guide to self-assessment is designed to help you become the kind of person you want to be, achieving the things you hope for, and understanding what and why things stand in your way. It will help you discover and develop in yourself the characteristics that separate the eagles from the ostriches.

You'll work on your ostrich as we work on Deirdre's and Walter's and Margaret's. You'll learn how to break free from the Ostrich Complex traps into which you've already fallen and easily avoid the others in your path. Then we'll move ahead to learn why the Ostrich Complex exists in your life and what specifically you can do about it.

Chapter 2

Stress in the Air, Head in the Sand

Now that we have pulled the Ostrich Complex from its lair to identify it, the key issue for us to look at now is: How does an Ostrich Complex develop? This general understanding will help you examine how your own Ostrich Complex developed, how you can trace it, and how you can design a prescription for escaping from it.

Deirdre Revisited. Let's discuss Deirdre's situation again. When I first met her I wondered, "Why is such a promising person having so much trouble completing her work?" Her new employers were giving her every opportunity to prove herself, to realize her full potential. And there lay the rub, as Shakespeare said. That's where Deirdre's problem began. The expectations for her success were high, so high that they were an intimidating challenge. For Deirdre that intimidation equaled paralysis.

As a legal aide, Deirdre had worked with a safety net. No sign saying "The buck stops here" hung over her desk. The results of her work were always in someone else's name, and her brilliant image could never be tarnished. She was overqualified for what she was doing, and therefore comfortable and secure.

Now Deirdre is on her own. Her work bears her signature. She is exposed to the scrutiny of the world. Deirdre is worried whether she can even perform as well as others do and as well as she is *supposed* to. She wonders, "Am I really as brilliant as they say I am?" The womblike shelter of her legal aide position is no longer there. Now she has to produce brilliant work, and she finds herself unable to meet that demand. Deirdre's problem has nothing to do with her ability to do good work. Inability is rarely the real problem with Ostrich Complex victims. Deirdre is afraid. Can she be as perfect as she feels she must be?

Deirdre is experiencing stress—a special type of stress at that. As we look at how her stress developed, we'll increase our understanding of the Ostrich Complex.

Stress and Our Behavior. When Deirdre was performing excellently as a legal aide, everything was under *control*. In fact, Deirdre was under control, the control of someone else. Even her reputation for being brilliant came from other people. Now that she is independent, her work quality and her reputation are under her own control. If something goes wrong and her work turns out to be less than brilliant, the responsibility cannot be shared, or even passed on to someone above her. The responsibility for perfection, or anything short of it, is hers alone.

Deirdre is suffering from the stress of suddenly becoming independent and all that it entails: responsibility, judgment, decisions, and more. She worries that she may have been brilliant only when others told her what to do. She secretly yearns for earlier times when she felt secure and unthreatened. Deirdre is afraid of not being perfect. Her fear is turning her into an ostrich, head in the sand, flanks exposed and vulnerable, with stress running through her like an electrical current. It is paralyzing her and putting her into danger.

If Deirdre does not perform better soon, she will lose her job. If she keeps her head in the sand and continues to let fear immobilize her, it is likely that her stress level will increase so much that she may break down emotionally. Her overwhelming need for perfection means that even if she muddles through at work, her performance will not be acceptable to her own standards.

Stress Affects Our Non-Behavior, Too. Stress in the Ostrich Complex serves as both stimulus and fodder. Stress sets up an environment that gives us permission to avoid discomfort. We fear how painful that stress will be if we have to face it head-on.

Stress has been described by many psychologists as "the illness of the eighties." It has been linked with everything from allergies and baldness to cancer, heart attack, and stroke, even to the likelihood that we will develop *future* illness. Its symptoms are well known to us all, and include anxiety, depression, and psychosomatic problems such as headaches, back pain, and stomach and gastrointestinal distress.

I want you to think about stress in a slightly different way. I'm adding the wrinkle that stress affects your *non-behavior* even more. I'll talk about that in a minute.

Right now, I want to share a bit more about what professionals have learned recently about stress. For example, one study reveals that emotional stress claims are becoming a "common cause of industrial disability" for everyone from executives to part-time workers.[2]

All of us have experienced the symptoms of stress. On more than one occasion we have seen their poison at work and at home. At work, such symptoms undermine productivity and drain the energy we need in order to cope with even simple tasks. It is a vicious cycle. The symptoms generated by the stress increase stress rather than relieving it.

You have a limited amount of energy to use in handling life's problems. If you expend it constantly in unconscious reactions to stress and fear, you can't have much left over to use in coping with actual problems. We are not bottomless pits of emotional and physical energy. When we ostrich the problems we have and allow stress to dominate our behavior, it depletes us and keeps us from accomplishing our goals. It initiates a cycle that works like this:

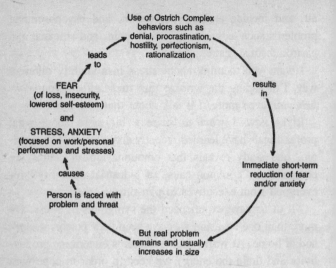

Use of Ostrich Complex
behaviors such as
denial, procrastination,
hostility, perfectionism,
rationalization

leads
to

FEAR
(of loss, insecurity,
lowered self-esteem)

and

STRESS, ANXIETY
(focused on work/personal
performance and stresses)

causes

Person is faced with
problem and threat

results
in

Immediate short-term
reduction of fear
and/or anxiety

But real problem
remains and usually
increases in size

THE OSTRICH COMPLEX CYCLE

The Threat. Deirdre had to face the possibility that she might not do perfect work. Glenn was faced with a threat from his boss. Margaret had to face the reality of being paid less than a colleague. Walter was threatened with loss of his job. And Roy constantly had to deal with the possiblity of losing Shirley.

In each case, the problem began with a threat. I think that you know these people well enough by now to say, "But some of these threats probably weren't real. Margaret wasn't going to get fired just because she asked her boss about her salary. Walter probably wasn't really training his replacement. And Roy never had Shirley's love to begin with, so what did he have to lose?"

Threats don't have to be real for the Ostrich Complex to develop—they just have to *feel* real. Children who won't let go of a teddy bear during the night because someone might come in and take it do not take lightly to the cold logic of reality that says, "Nobody else would want a battered old teddy bear like mine." Teenagers who cling to a fad because they will lose all their popularity if they act independently don't care about parental logic. And adults who are faced with the imagined loss of a job, self-esteem or someone's love don't care for a dose of reality from a friend. The imagined threat is just as terrifying as a real one might be—perhaps more so. That's why I asked you earlier to pay attention to ostrich behaviors in your friends. It's much easier to see the effects of imagined threats in them than in ourselves.

Some threats *are* real. Deirdre cannot meet everyone's expectations—particularly her own. Walter may have to deal with the possibility that the company is planning to let him go. You and I have to deal with real problems every day, as trivial as losing money in a vending machine, as embarrassing as being glared at for being late to an appointment, as miserable as an unpleasant relationship at work or at home.

Think for a minute about the real threatening situations and problems that you've had to deal with in the last twenty-four hours. I'll bet that your list ranges from minor things such as a traffic jam on the way to work to major ones such as an argument with your boss or spouse. There's nothing wrong with being able to generate a good, long list. In fact, being able to list those threats is an excellent early step toward effective handling of the Ostrich Complex.

The Stress. Each of these problems, the real and the imaginary ones, causes stress and fear. The Ostrich Complex victim reacts to stress by focusing on himself, on his own experience of the stress, rather than on the source of that stress. He or she becomes anxious rather than angry, fearful rather than forthright when facing a problem.

Take Roy's situation, for example. When Shirley continued to refuse his requests for a talk about their relationship, he could have become angry. He could have confronted Shirley with his request for a serious discussion about where they stood. And he could have handled this confrontation without getting Shirley angry if he honestly expressed his confusion about her double messages, if he opened up about the hurt he felt each time she rejected him for someone or something else. Expressing our real, inside feelings and confusion rarely makes the other person angry. More often it helps clear up the situation. When Roy swallowed his own feelings, he turned the anger and doubt onto himself rather than onto Shirley's behavior and the situation.

Each time he thought about confronting Shirley and gaining a clearer understanding of their relationship, Roy experienced a high degree of stress. There were parts of that understanding that he just did not want to face and have to acknowledge as reality. He made an ostrich's choice—he opted for a draining anxiety instead of a devastating truth. It's a delaying tactic destined to fail.

The Fear. Some dangers *are* real; some just *feel* real. Either one can trigger ostrich behavior because *perceived* danger produces fear. In fact, it is the only immediate trigger.

Roy's danger is real. In his heart he *knows* Shirley will not commit herself to a relationship and, in insisting, he may lose her. That is too tough and frightening a risk for him to take.

Margaret's worry centers on having to confront her boss and risk being told that she's not as good as her colleagues. Fear keeps Walter all bottled up, his stress ballooning to a point where he's suffering major physical problems and losing his effectiveness at work. His threat *feels* real, but just might not be. If he complains to his friends about Jessica's being trained to replace him and it's not true, he will look quite the paranoid. If he views it as a *real* threat, it becomes too imposing to handle; it makes him more insecure and reduces his already low self-esteem. So Walter tries to forget the problem, worries about it even more, and then tries to forget it even harder.

If there were no fears, there would be no ostriches. We would all be eagles soaring above our problems, dealing with them easily and effectively, never allowing anyone to impose his will on us when it differed from our own desires. The world has few eagles and many ostriches. We are humans, not birds. We cannot fly above our troubles nor hide from them; we must face them.

Ostrich Spells R-e-l-i-e-f. Why do so many of us use ostrich behaviors to deal with our fears and anxieties? As you can see in the diagram, ostrich behaviors are effective in making us feel better about the situation *for a short time*. What seems like a solution really compounds the problem.

Glenn, for example, is a *collector.* Just like someone who collects stamps or saves string, Glenn collects negative feelings about himself. Each time something similar to the present run-in with his boss, Mr. Stevens, occurs, Glenn takes note of what a failure he is. Those bad feelings don't go away; instead, they simmer, just below boiling in the same way the contents of a pot stay hot on the stove. Glenn also doesn't forget that it was Mr. Stevens who made him feel that way.

Collecting is one of the most dangerous ostrich behaviors where relationships are concerned. "She holds grudges" and "He never forgets any criticism" represent the types of accusations I hear all too often from couples having relationship problems. And employees, like Glenn, also collect until their sacks can't hold any more. First, the anger leaks out; then, as though it's a complete surprise to them, the bag bursts and the hostility gushes.

Some of us like Roy totally *deny* the problem, and by denying its importance, we diminish the accompanying threat and stress. When we deny the reality of a problem, we lie to ourselves and to those who are involved in our problem. As our parents told us, lies will always catch up with us.

Others use the tried and true technique of *procrastination*, putting off until tomorrow what *needs* to be done today. Let's see how long you can go without paying your phone bill or, even better, your rent or house payment. If you ever have, it probably didn't take too long for you to realize that it is not an effective way to save money. After a free ride for a month or two, you found yourself without a phone or a place to live, and/or penalties or interest to pay to boot.

Deirdre, on the other hand, is a *perfectionist*. She can find hundreds of reasons for not finishing her work, but the bottom line is that she is afraid of being rejected if her work isn't perfect. She is supposed to be brilliant. Deirdre's problem reminds me of the sad story of a teenager I knew. School grades came out; she got all As except for one B. In her suicide note, she wrote, "If I fail in what I do, I fail in what I am."

Perfectionists live all around us. "If I can't live in a palace, I'll just stay in this dump." "If I can't date someone perfect, I just won't go out with anyone at all." Or how about, "If I can't get just the right job, I won't work at all."

Relief Spelled S-h-o-r-t T-e-r-m. The relief provided us by our ostrich behaviors is short-lived. It's like turning on the air conditioner in a room that's on fire. It feels good—for a while. The real problem, the threat and the fear, remain, and sooner or later return to haunt us. Only now, what was a relatively minor problem has become a formidable one.

Remember those times when you've had a bad tooth and have taken an aspirin or two for the pain? The pills provided *temporary* relief, but when the medication wore off, the pain returned, usually feeling worse than when you first noticed it. You can take all the aspirin you want, but at some point you'll have to treat that tooth. The unfortunate part is that most of us have learned maladaptive ways, such as collecting, denying, perfectionism, and procrastination, to reduce unpleasant feelings, and are willing to take short-term relief instead of going for the more permanent—but more risky—solution.

Let me introduce you to two new people, Nancy and Nick, and let their story show you how the Ostrich Complex cycle works, how one inappropriate response to problems leads to another.

The Ostrich Cycle: Nancy and Nick Style. Nancy and Nick were the perfect couple. In fact, they had been considered the perfect couple for so long that the image of perfection became one of their root problems. Perfect couples never have problems. Right?

Their romance was ideal. Nick was already a vice-president of a major import-export company when he and Nancy met. Nancy had spent a few years playing with the beautiful people in various parts of the world but was now looking forward to settling down. A job with great potential dropped into her lap, and she rose rapidly in the advertising industry to become an important account executive. The match between Nancy and Nick was made in heaven. Success and happiness lapped at their heels when they were in public just as their Saint Bernard did when they were at home. Friends did indeed view them as the perfect couple.

But as the years went by, Nancy started putting on weight. She's now openly unhappy about it, and complains that it's due to her job, which keeps her sitting for most of the day. She's also very bothered that Nick seems to look exactly as he did when they met, possibly even better, and she is reminded of the fact, daily it seems, by her friends. Nancy remembers all too well how Nick valued her looks when they were first married. He even boasted about her figure.

Gaining weight has made Nancy anxious and insecure, and no business success can offset her fears. She is threatened by the possible loss of Nick's love—perhaps even the loss of Nick himself. She has taken up an exercise program in order to trim down, but it is hard to find the time and the energy, so the program remains a halfhearted one. Nothing seems to work.

As you can guess, Nick has been growing more distant. There seems to be less evening and weekend time for them to spend together. He says it's due to the demands of his work. Nancy worries that it's another woman. She spends much of her time looking for the telltale signs that he's having an affair but has said nothing to him. The result has been that her exercise program and diet have become even more difficult to handle. Instead, she brings work home and nibbles as she works. Each time this happens, she blames Nick—"If Nick were here, I wouldn't have to eat and work because we could do something together"— collecting anger toward him with each page of work and bite of food.

But what about Nick? He has noticed Nancy's increasing dedication to food. It's annoyed him, particularly since he had already been bothered by Nancy's growing bulges and weight problem. He also has been collecting some anger at her lack of time with him. A little more anger filled his sack each time Nancy had to miss an evening with him because of a business appointment; or when she had to leave town for a few days to give a presentation; or on those occasions when something came up and she said, "Oh, Nick, I'm sure you understand. Business, you know." Each incident made him upset, but he chose to avoid "nagging" and never discussed his concerns with her.

Nick has chosen to try to overlook the problems, denying how bothered he is by where he feels Nancy places him on her list of priorities. Instead of discussing his disappointment and hurt with Nancy, he has spent more time out with the boys. He feels awkward about discussing Nancy's weight problem with her, and begins to feel like a little boy wanting his mommy when he thinks about telling her of his concerns about her priorities.

Neither will discuss their fears and the stress in their relationship with anyone else. After all, they're the perfect couple.

What really has happened to Nancy and Nick? The answer is that they share an Ostrich Complex. They share the use of denial to ease the pain for a little while, falling into the "after all, we're the perfect couple" view that so many have smothered them with over the years. And each is collecting many hurt feelings, reading the other's behavior as, "You aren't important to me anymore." Each one's self-esteem is low, and they can find very little security in their once happy relationship.

Nancy and Nick's Shared Ostrich: Analyzed. Let's look at how Nick and Nancy moved through the steps of the Ostrich Complex cycle. It's difficult to say exactly what the first threat in the relationship was or when it occurred. Most likely it came when each began realizing that the love felt for the other was not as strong as it once was. As a result, symptoms of their reaction to the threat began to appear. Nancy put on weight and started spending more time at work or bringing work home. Nick's response centered on nights out with the boys—an effective way to avoid having to deal with his fears about the relationship. These symptoms also dealt a telling blow to their shared but unspoken worry about being the "perfect couple." Both know that that is no longer true, and maybe never was, but neither wants to pull that cover away and examine the real problems.

The real problem, their failure to make their love and commitment to each other a top priority, is the internal threat in this shared Ostrich Complex. For Nick and Nancy, the internal threat involves their personal thoughts and feelings of helplessness, self-doubt, and insecurity. Those feelings are basic to the problems they have and are basic to the stress that keeps their ostrich behavior alive.

More About the Internal Threat. The Ostrich Complex may take the form of denial, collecting, procrastination, or perfectionism. We aim it at reducing the *internal* threat we feel. Nancy and Nick deny the existence of a real problem in order to save their mutual image as the perfect couple. Their behavior is not at all aimed at solving the basic problems in their relationship. Neither is willing to confront the fear of losing the other. They are classic ostriches.

Most ostriches follow the same path. They focus on the external symptoms, rather than confronting the real internal problem. Let's take a brief look at what those internal fears in general tend to be and what external situations seem to bring them out in us.

Alan, a friend of mine, gives us a good example. He's someone with whom I've shared many of these ideas over the years.

All of us know that the most effective salespeople are cool and in control. They can negotiate with the toughest customers without breaking into a sweat. Right? Alan believed this, too. He wanted to be the best. Any less than that was unacceptable.

To understand why anything less than perfection was

unacceptable to Alan, you'd also have to know his parents and get a glimpse of their expectations of him. Both Alan's mom and dad were highly regarded corporate lawyers, and for years were certain that their talented son would follow in their footsteps. But Alan followed another path. As children often do, Alan chose a career almost opposite to his parents' hopes. He fights a constant battle trying to prove himself to them and to himself—only achieving perfection will tell him he made the right decision.

One morning when he found his hands shaking and his palms sweating as he waited in the reception area before his appointment with a company president, he began having doubts about his ability to play in the big leagues. After all, over $1 million in sales was at stake in that single meeting, and this was the biggest potential sale of his young career. Alan came close to turning himself into an ostrich in just a few unhappy moments.

He was more worried about himself than about getting the job done. The threat was more self-doubt than fear of what the president would decide, but Alan was luckier than most potential ostriches. Long before this meeting, he'd spent time examining his need for perfectionism. He was ready for situations such as this one when fears and self-doubt struck. He still, however, almost ostriched his deal away.

His "look-out, you're ostriching" signal came a moment before he was ushered in to the meeting. Afraid that his nervousness would make him look foolish, almost ready to excuse himself from the meeting before he even walked in, Alan overheard two secretaries talking about him. Their comments ranged from ones about his suit to how icy cool and confident he looked sitting there.

Alan realized at that moment that no one else had noticed how nervous he was—it was all inside his head. He was able to put the incident into the perspective of issues that we'd discussed and that he'd thought about. To his credit, Alan was able to convert his realization that he was sliding into ostrich behavior to his immediate advantage and see that most of his fears were imagined ones. He summoned up his newly buoyed courage and laughed at himself for having come so close to blowing it (humor often helps keeps the ostrich at bay). He then breezed through the meeting successfully without a single nervous twitch. And to make the story even sweeter, Alan today is the top salesman in his company, most of the time practicing what I preach much better than I do.

Let's turn to Walter. Afraid of losing his job to Jessica, he has not been as insightful as Alan. The anxiety he felt about Jessica's real purpose in the office developed into self-doubts about his own security. That stress led him to worry about his ability even to assess the situation accurately. The additional stress, in turn, led to a total block on his ability to do his work well. He could not even feel comfortable sharing such fears with anyone else. If he could have confronted those self-doubts, examined the situation accurately, and shared his fears with others, Walter could have eased the stress and escaped being an ostrich.

And what about Margaret, so afraid to ask her boss about her salary? What is she hiding from? The fear of being fired? Hardly. That might be a frightening possibility if she were doing poorly in her work, but that's not the case. She won't get fired for asking for a raise or equal pay, but she could get rejected. Her boss could say no. He could tell her that she isn't worth any more money. In essence, he could deliver a blow to her ego. Margaret isn't willing to take that risk. She keeps trying to ignore the situation, collecting bits of anger at her boss, her colleague, and her work, rather than taking the step of putting who she is out there at risk.

In each of these situations, it isn't the external problem that poses the greatest threat, but rather how each person interprets it internally. If the problem hits us where we feel the most vulnerable, we want to run and hide. If it hits us in the spot that we work so hard to keep protected, it's not surprising to see the fear trigger the first stages of the Ostrich Complex.

The Subtle Ostrich. I've talked a lot about the major behaviors that all of us use as part of the Ostrich Complex, including denial, collecting, procrastination, and perfectionism. There are also some basic, widespread maneuvers that are not so readily recognized as ostriching, but are often ways of hiding: rationalization, hostility, and even depression.

Many of us use these behaviors as normal parts of our everyday lives, often when no ostrich is lurking in the bushes. How do we then tell when these tactics are manifestations of the Ostrich Complex or when they are normal, often healthy ways of dealing with everyday life? The key to such a separation, to uncovering the ostrich behind the various camouflages it likes to use, is to ask one basic question: *If it weren't for* _____ (fill this in with whatever the masking behavior is, e.g., "depression"), *what would I be able to accomplish?*

Let's ask that question for some of the ostriches we've come to know.

- If it weren't for *her perfectionism*, Deirdre would be able to *complete the work on her case* and find out how brilliant she really is.
- If it weren't for *his collecting*, Glenn would be able *to handle situations* that cause him self-doubt and the anger that he swallows.
- If she weren't *procrastinating* for fear of learning an unpleasant truth, Margaret would be able *to ask her boss for a raise* and find out how much he really values her.
- If it weren't for *his denial*, Roy would be able *to free himself from his relationship* with Shirley and move his love-life ahead.
- And Nancy and Nick? If it weren't for *their mutual denial and fear* of not being the perfect couple, they would be able *to move beyond an adolescent model of a relationship* into one based on an accurate understanding of each other and an openness about their love and fears.

The Untouched Threat. Have you ever forgotten to pay a $10 parking ticket? Well, you were warned that if you delay paying, fines and penalities will be attached to it. Then one day when you least expect it you get pulled over by a police officer who wants to tell you that your tail lights are out. He runs a routine check on your license only to discover that there is now an outstanding warrant for over $100. Suddenly you wish you'd paid the ticket much earlier. As he's hauling you in, the $10 seems small compared to the mess in which you now find yourself.

While we're letting the Ostrich Complex tie up so much of our energies avoiding the threat we feel, the real external problem remains unresolved. External problems just don't go away when we don't deal with them. They either just sit on our doorstep waiting to catch us as soon as we venture outside the safety of our house, or they run around the block growing in size while we pretend that they've really gone away for good.

Even when it causes no major life threat, the Ostrich Complex drains off a surprisingly large amount of our vitality, leaving us just enough of ourselves to continue sustaining the complex. For some, those at the extreme of the Ostrich Complex, the paralysis is devastating. It takes them through life as though they were in a zombielike state, leaving them totally at the mercy of their ostrich.

So What Now? Although there are many ways to cope with problems at work, in relationships, in striving for personal goals, and in dealing with the hassles of daily life, the behavior patterns we develop to address all of these different areas are often consistent. More often than not, whether we use denial or become creative collectors, bumping into the same problem over and over tells us that there is an ostrich lurking nearby.

Remember that by its very nature the Ostrich Complex does not exist out in the open. It has to masquerade as some other problem. That is why its manifestations are so various, why its plumage is so rich in variety. In some ways an Ostrich Complex adapts itself to us much as a chameleon adapts its coloration to its surroundings.

Because we are all individuals, the Ostrich Complex arises for each of us in a different way, responding to our individual circumstances. The only thing that you can count on with an ostrich is that it will always want to remain hidden.

Now that we know what the Ostrich Complex looks like and how it acts, the next step is to find it within ourselves. Since the ostrich is, after all, a master of disguise, how can we know which of *our* problems are due to the Ostrich Complex?

That discovery is our next goal. We'll identify the size, location, and temperament of our own pet ostrich. To do this, we must examine an assortment of our reactions and behaviors. We can then see what our patterns are and then be well on our way to seeing the ostrich behind the pattern.

That's the purpose of the Ostrich Complex Checklist in the next chapter. It is a teaching tool that allows you to compute your overall Ostrich Quotient. It will also show you how to map out the relative strengths of the basic patterns that make up your Ostrich Complex. The checklist is easy to fill out—some have even called it fun. Since you've read these first two chapters, the ostrich is practically in the bag. Happy hunting!

Chapter 3

The Ostrich Complex Inventory

Ostrich behaviors help—for a little while. Remember how neither Nancy nor Nick wanted to worry about their relationship and how Margaret refused to examine her anxiety about her position in the company. Ostrich behaviors help by defending us against those uncomfortable, often painful, feelings of worry, fear, and anxiety.

The reason we do what we do—or don't do—is pretty basic. We just don't like to feel pain, mental or physical. Freud's view was that our defense against such pain is unconscious, the result of some automatic system that cycles into action when the pain gets too great. We don't think about defending ourselves, he would argue, we just do it. It's a concept similar to that used in fuses or circuit breakers; when the current gets too great, the system automatically shuts off as a means of protection against overload.

Most of us in psychology today view such defenses against pain as susceptible to a person's voluntary control. I don't mean that we set out to defend against anxiety in a premeditated way as much as we allow ourselves to use habits to deal with certain situations when they get too stressful. We do things that we've learned will work and will help us feel safer or at least better.

The tolerance level for pain in some people allows only a little to get through and then shuts down quickly and completely. Others can stand a lot before any defense needs to come to their rescue. Not only do the ways in which we defend against the pain vary among people, but nearly all of the defenses we use make up some part of the Ostrich Complex.

These defenses make the Ostrich Complex harder for us to identify within ourselves. I've used words like *masquerade* and *disguise* to show you how obscured the Ostrich Complex can be. In this chapter we find a way to clear away some of the camouflage that surrounds the ostrich in your life. That's what the upcoming inventory is all about.

It is essential that you identify your typical response to the stresses, fears, and anxieties of daily life. It's essential that you become aware of how big a role the Ostrich Complex plays in your life and what specific aspects of it fit into your habitual way of responding—defending—in stressful situations.

The Ostrich Complex Inventory is a set of forty questions that ask you to think about the way you generally behave and feel in a variety of situations. Your response to the questions will probably be a bit similar to that of

Marge, a recent client, so I'm going to give you the rationale that I gave Marge (and that I give all my clients whenever I ask them to take a psychological test). The temptation is to lie a little (fudge?) when you answer the questions. After all, they're pretty personal, and it's natural to want to skim over your problems and think about more pleasant things. But who is asking the questions? *You!* And who will see the answers? *You!* And what do you have to gain by fudging your answers even a little bit? *Nothing!*

Sure it's hard to examine what makes us tick, particularly when the ticking may signal some kind of time bomb problem that we're afraid may go off. But imagine what part of you will be hurt if that bomb does go off next to you and you've got your head—or more—buried in the sand. If by pulling your head out of the sand and by taking an honest look at yourself you can see and defuse that time bomb, won't life be a lot better?

So read each question and answer it honestly. *After* you respond to the Inventory, we'll discuss both what your overall score and your specific ostrich behavior scores mean. Note that the scoring for the Inventory is in two parts and follows the answer sheet.

THE OSTRICH COMPLEX INVENTORY

HOW TO USE THE INVENTORY

Use the Answer Sheet on page 62 or remove one of the Inventory Answer Sheets from the appendix section, pages

237–239. Several copies of the Answer Sheet are provided so that you can take the Inventory again at some future time. Answer each of the questions by using the 1 to 5 scale shown, putting your choice of numbers in the appropriate place on the Answer Sheet.

The Ostrich Complex Inventory presents you with forty statements that describe behavior or attitudes. Read each one and determine the extent to which it reflects *your* characteristics. Remember, this Inventory is about *your* ostrich, not your boss's, nor your lover's, nor your mechanic's. Next, choose a number that matches your response from the scale below, and write that number in the space provided on the answer sheet. After you have answered all of the questions, turn the page to find your score.

SCORING FORMAT: Keep these words and numbers in mind as you respond to each statement.

Totally Unlike Me	Very Little Like Me	Equally Like And Unlike Me	Very Much Like Me	Totally Like Me
1	2	3	4	5

THE OSTRICH COMPLEX INVENTORY

1. I get irritated with myself when I make simple mistakes.

2. I don't believe that a friend of mine could intentionally hurt me, because all of my friends are essentially good people.

3. I like to go over old love letters, photographs, and remembrances of past loves, even ones that turned out unpleasantly.

4. When I had to turn in a paper at school, I stayed up the night before to write it.

5. I will often tear up a letter rather than send it if it contains a minor error.

6. It's okay to think positive, but I think it's essential to recognize problems and take direct steps to overcome them.

7. I can easily express my feelings to someone who has done something to hurt me.

8. I miss a lot of excellent opportunities because I do not act on good tips when I first get them.

9. I will spend extra hours on a project in order to get it exactly right.

10. Like Will Rogers, I never met a person I didn't like.

11. I can enumerate the ways in which certain people have hurt me.

12. I spend a large portion of my time making to-do lists.

13. I like to jump right into a new project. If I'm not sure how to do it when I start, I'll know how by the time I'm done.

14. If my lover or mate were to give me clear signals about dumping me for someone else, I would stick to routine as if everything were the same as before.

15. I remember many unpleasant things done to me when I was a child that I felt helpless about at the time.

16. Although I plan to take vacations, I always seem too busy to leave town.

17. Even though I don't like to, I feel a lot of pressure to work on things until I get them "just right."

18. Very few people have satisfactory sexual relationships, so I don't worry about it since there are plenty of other pleasures in life.

19. I keep a mental list of mistakes committed by anyone who has gotten ahead at my expense or who has treated me unfairly.

20. I'm usually on time for appointments.

21. I know that many of the things I do could be done better, but usually it's not worth the extra time to make those small changes.

22. I believe that if you don't *think* that you have problems, then you don't; it's thinking that you do that gets you into trouble.

23. I have at least one friend who frequently says unkind things to me. One of these days he/she will go too far.

24. I find that I worry so much about getting things done on time that it makes them take even longer to get done.

25. I'd rather take the bus or walk rather than drive around in an unattractive or inferior make of car.

26. When I'm rejected, I get upset and demand an explanation, refusing to go away until I get one.

27. It is difficult for me to remember things that people have done to upset me.

28. There are bills I don't pay until I'm threatened or penalized with interest charges.

29. I'd rather finish a job and move on to something else than get stuck endlessly trying to improve it.

30. I've been told that I deal directly with conflicts and give them concentration and attention until they're resolved.

31. I often feel that my boss (lover, friend, whoever) is pushing me to the end of my rope, and if he/she does just one more unpleasant thing to me, I am going to end our relationship.

32. I'm often found rushing around at the last minute tying up loose ends.

33. Friends tell me that I'm easygoing and flexible when it comes to day-to-day activities.

34. When someone close to me confronts me with my own inadequacies I find myself turning the argument around and criticizing him/her.

35. Even after someone has betrayed me, it's easy for me to forgive and forget.

36. I only go to the doctor or dentist when it's an emergency or when the problem can't wait any longer.

37. There have been times when I've needed to complete a project but found myself still wanting to get it "just a little bit better" even when I had to stop.

38. There have been times when problems have sneaked up on me without my having any idea they were developing.

39. I keep a detailed diary.

40. I always send birthday and Christmas cards early enough so that they'll arrive on time.

THE OSTRICH COMPLEX INVENTORY

ANSWER SHEET

Totally Unlike Me	Very Little Like Me	Equally Like And Unlike Me	Very Much Like Me	Totally Like Me
1	2	3	4	5

Answer each of the questions by selecting the appropriate number from the scale above and writing that number below. Some of the questions will be more difficult to answer than others but answer each one as best you can. After you've answered all forty questions, read the directions below on how to score your Ostrich Complex Inventory.

Perfectionism	Denial	Collecting	Procrastination
1. _____	2. _____	3. _____	4. _____
5. _____	6. _][_*	7. _][_*	8. _____
9. _____	10._____	11._____	12._____
13._][_*	14._____	15._____	16._____
17._____	18._____	19._____	20._][_*
21._][_*	22._____	23._____	24._____
25._____	26._][_*	27._][_*	28._____
29._][_*	30._][_*	31._____	32._____
33._][_*	34._____	35._][_*	36:_____
37._____	38._____	39._____	40._][_*

[   ] + [   ] + [   ] + [   ] = _____
  1   2   3   4   OQ

HOW TO SCORE THE OSTRICH COMPLEX INVENTORY

First, let me point out that your score for twelve of the forty questions needs to be reversed. For example, question six as stated measures a non-denial attitude. To get your *denial* attitude for that question, you must reverse the answer scale. For questions 6, 7, 13, 20, 21, 26, 27, 29, 30, 33, 35, and 40 (these items have a * next to their space on the answer key with a][dividing the space into halves), **reverse** your score as follows:

> If you put a 5, cross it out and put 1
> If you put a 4, cross it out and put 2
> If you put a 3, leave it as 3
> If you put a 2, cross it out and put 4
> If you put a 1, cross it out and put 5

Now add **down** each of the four columns and put the total *for that column* inside the brackets provided. You will end up with four totals, each of which can range from 10 to 50. After you have computed the totals for each of the four columns, add across those four numbers and place that total on the line above the letters "OQ." Transfer each of these numbers to the appropriate places on the graph on page 69 and follow the directions for the graph.

HOW TO INTERPRET YOUR SCORE

You received two different sets of scores from the Inventory. One set is made up of the four numbers you just transferred to the graph on page 69. Each of these numbers (as you will read) represents how large a role each of the four primary ostrich behaviors plays in your life. The second score is your overall Ostrich Quotient—your OQ. To compute your own OQ, you added across the four boxes at the bottom of the columns. That number, which you put on the line marked "OQ," can range from 40 to 200 and is your overall Ostrich Complex score.

Your Ostrich Quotient. This score serves as a summary for you where your overall ostrich behaviors are concerned. As we discussed earlier, a particular daily problem may cause you to respond with an ostrich behavior specific to that incident. Roy may be assertive, clear, and forthright with his colleagues at work, but let him start dealing in emotional relationships with women and look out for trouble. Taking Roy's case one step further, when he does respond with ostrich behaviors, we've learned that he uses denial more than any other. He procrastinates when it comes to actually discussing the problem with Shirley, but his primary mode of handling their relationship is with denial. He might not score a high OQ but he probably would knock the top off the denial scale.

Let's take the interpretation of the OQ further by discussing the various groupings on the OQ scale and what they mean in terms of ostrich behavior.

Very Low (60 and below): Pardon me for asking, but did someone give you this book as a gift? If you've answered the questions honestly, your score is saying that the Ostrich Complex rarely—no, never—is a problem for you. You're scoring like the effective doers-not-talkers I mentioned earlier. But you still have a choice as to what you do with such a forthright manner. On the one hand, you can be a great model for those around you, using your sensitivity to help others learn better ways to deal with their own ostrich problems. But you can be pretty intimidating to them as well. Imagine what kind of a difficult goal your behavior sets for a perfectionist who seeks to emulate you! And can a collector be open with you and tell you that you've done something upsetting to him? Use your lack of ostrich behavior wisely and many will have you to thank for their improvement.

Low (61–100): A nice score, suggesting that, overall, the Ostrich Complex is not standing in the way of an effective and enjoyable life. Let me repeat that one word, *overall*, however. Even scoring in this range, it's possible to show extreme non-ostrich behavior in three of the four scales and still have one scale that for you is a major ostrich problem. Examine whether you're low across all areas or whether there is one in which you scored higher than you would like. If you have scored very high in one area but low in the other three, you've probably got excellent skills to use in bringing about positive change.

Medium (101–140): Note that I don't use the word *average* to describe scores in this range. I couldn't do that and then emphasize how individual the Ostrich Complex is. Your score here means that overall—there's that word again—your Ostrich Complex falls in the medium range of intensity. I know few people, however, who score medium across all four behavior areas. Most score low in one or two and high in the others. Pay particular attention to two of your behavior pattern scores, your highest and your lowest. Ask yourself, "Why the difference?" Think about what internal threats exist in your highest area that you can manage to control in situations involving your lowest scale. Does a fear of being rejected if you're not perfect trigger the perfectionism scale, although your denial scale is low because you pride yourself on having a realistic view of the rest of the world? You can learn some things from the effective way you handle situations involving your lowest scales.

High (141–175): The atmosphere begins to get thin the higher you go in this range. But, unfortunately, the ostrich thrives in such rarified air. Scores here reflect a person who has adopted the Ostrich Complex as a way of life. You use two, three, or even four of the primary ostrich patterns; and, I would speculate, you use them almost as a package. That's how we saw Walter using his ostrich behaviors, denying problems for a while, then putting off dealing with them, and then collecting negative feelings and anger because he was receiving so little support. If you've scored here, you couldn't have made a better decision than to pick up this book and tackle the ostrich in your life. Stick with it.

Very High (176 and above): It's as difficult to score in this range as it is to score in the very low range. Your score here reveals that in coping with life you ostrich time after time, almost without rest. And from the fatigue that results from using your energy and vitality just to support an Ostrich Complex, other psychological symptoms have developed. Very high scorers also show extensive feelings of depression, helplessness, and even hopelessness that accompany their anxiety responses to stress. It's not a pleasant way to live each day, working hard, as Alice in Wonderland did, just to keep from falling further behind. Let me say two things to you here. First, you deserve a lot of credit for being willing to tackle problems that at times may seem insurmountable. Second, go slowly. The successes will come, but don't quit if they don't come as fast as you want now that you've decided to tackle your many ostriches. Yours is truly a case where slow and steady will win the race.

Your Own Ostrich Behavior Scores. As you responded to the statements on the inventory, you no doubt noticed a few things. First, you noticed that many of the conditions were more true for you than were others. Second, you saw how varied are the ways in which we face anxiety each day. In addition, you observed that several themes ran through the forty statements. I'm sure I confirmed this latter observation for you when the instructions told you to add down the columns and finish up with four scores that were totaled into the Ostrich Quotient.

Each of the columns corresponds to one of the four primary behaviors that make up the Ostrich Complex. These four, *perfectionism, denial, collecting,* and *procrastination,* are, at the same time, symptoms of the complex and problems in their own right. It's important for us to take our definitions a bit further now and understand each of these well if we are to agree on the best ways to change ostrich behavior.

Where Did You Score? We can also place our scores for each of the four ostrich behaviors on a continuum from very low to very high. Let's look at that range of scores and the appropriate breakdowns here, before we move into a discussion of each specific pattern.

To do this, use the graph on page 69 to record your scores. If you haven't done so already, take each ostrich behavior score from your answer sheet and record that number in the appropriate place on the graph page. Then, shade in each column up to where your score falls. Notice that the columns are marked to indicate the intensity of that particular ostrich behavior for you. For example, a score of 40 puts you solidly in the *high* range for that behavior, while a score of 16 is near the bottom of the *low* range.

Use the graph to get an idea of the relative position each of your ostrich behaviors has assumed in your life. As you read the discussion for each, keep in mind how intense that specific one is for you. To make this a bit easier, I've even left a space at the beginning of each section for you to record your score.

I know that this section might be getting a bit dry, a bit lacking in pizzazz, but stick with me. I'm using some psychology on you—and not trying to keep it a secret. I know that if we can come to an agreement about what each of these behavior patterns really is and what it does in our lives, and then move on to a discussion of where your own ostrich calls home, changing those patterns will be all the easier. You may be tempted to jump ahead—it's okay to have that enthusiasm. It's great energy for change; but walk with me a bit longer and then the path for your final dash will be flat and clear.

OSTRICH COMPLEX SCORING GRAPH

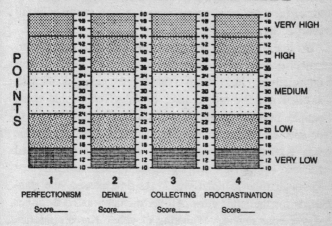

1	2	3	4
PERFECTIONISM	DENIAL	COLLECTING	PROCRASTINATION
Score___	Score___	Score___	Score___

Instructions: Copy your scores for each of the four ostrich behaviors into the appropriate spaces. Then shade in the correct amount of the column corresponding to each score. This makes it easy to see at a glance which ostrich behaviors are the most significant for you. Then read on.

OSTRICH BEHAVIOR PATTERNS

Perfectionism. [score: ____] This is perhaps the most subtle of ostrich styles. Some perfectionists deceive themselves into believing that they really are too good for some of the tasks that must be done. As a result, the tasks don't get done and the perfectionist gets labelled as irresponsible. Other perfectionists set standards for themselves that no one could possibly meet. I told you the sad story earlier of the teenager who committed suicide because of one grade of *B* on her report card. These perfectionists spend a lot of time feeling depressed because they continually fall short of the unrealistic goals they've set for themselves.

A third group of perfectionists often masquerade as procrastinators, twiddling their tasks away. Behind their dilly-dallying, however, is a fear that they can't do the task as well as they would like. Look at the trouble some people have with the simple task of writing notes to parents or writing thank-you notes after birthdays. That was Karen's complaint. Karen was constantly stressed because she put off writing to her mother until she had "enough time to do it well." As time passed, the standards for the letter grew. All her mother wanted from her was a note saying, "Thinking of you." Karen's internal demands, however, said the letter had to be perfect.

Denial. [score: _____] Denial, in essence, means lying to ourselves. It is a popular way to hide from the threats around us. It's true that we can sometimes use denial as a normal accommodation to things that we really cannot change.[3, 4] But it's rare that denial is the best way for us to confront a problem. Haven't you ever fouled up and placed the blame on someone else, convincing yourself that it really was that person's fault?

And what about little disappointments? When you didn't get into your first choice of colleges or get offered *the* job you wanted, any chance it wasn't your fault at all? Or any chance you just shrugged your shoulders and said, "Well, I didn't really want that anyhow." That's denial, and it's classic ostrich behavior. Look at what that does to your ability to change for the better and deal with that kind of problem in the future. It puts emotional shackles around you just as firmly as those on the legs of someone in a chain gang. Often we deny the very existence of annoying situations that we are afraid to confront, hoping they will go away on their own. Poof! How often does that magic happen?

Collecting. [Score: _____] I've told you something about collecting already. I pointed out how often in my clinical practice I hear about the consequences of collecting complaints, ones such as, "She's still angry at something that happened five years ago," and, "I never knew that it bothered him until one day he said he was leaving." Our friends Glenn and Roy are collectors. It is likely that neither will really forgive the people in their lives who are causing them so much stress. They're storing up their anger instead of releasing it appropriately at the right time.

The collector likes to tell himself, "If this happens one more time, I'll really let him know how I feel." Of course it happens one more time and the collector keeps collecting. It's similar to what I see between parents and children in grocery stores. You know the scene: Mom says, "No candy"; the child screams; Mom says, "If you do that one more time I'll . . ." Ten times later neither the threat nor the child's behavior has changed. You see, the collector rarely translates threats into action. Doing is too scary, so the collector talks, building security and reducing anxiety— temporarily.

Procrastination. [score: _____] This behavior pattern appears to be the all-time ostrich favorite. It's so easy to put off things that entail discomfort. Because they don't hurt very much at the moment, we postpone unpleasant tasks and obligations even to the point of endangering health.

You understand that there are potential health problems if you don't go to the doctor or dentist regularly. But you put off your check-ups. Then why be surprised when Margaret delays going to her boss, or when Walter can't seem to get to go in for a talk about his concerns? Most of us procrastinate—at least a little bit.

My observation is that we do our worst procrastination on those very things that can make the biggest difference to our lives. The small tasks that others assign us are not so hard to accomplish. It's those wonderful projects that we assign to ourselves, projects that will help us achieve what we want to achieve and become the person we want to be, that increase the intensity of the stress-fear-procrastination process. Your score on this scale can give you a good idea of how much procrastination is involved in your own Ostrich Complex.

These four behaviors are the identifying marks of the Ostrich Complex. You know how the Ostrich Complex looks and feels. And you know how you use it in trying to reduce the stress in your own life. The Ostrich Complex draws from each of us a camouflage of its own. It develops uniquely as we deal with problems at home or problems at work. Where in your life does the ostrich choose to bury its head? You are ready to narrow your search.

PART TWO

The Care and Feeding of an Ostrich Complex

Chapter 4

Where Your Ostrich Calls Home

Most of us spend one third of our lives asleep. Add to that the percentage of time we keep our heads in the ground, and what's left? Not much. How much energy does *your* Ostrich Complex drain each day? And what could you be doing with that energy if you had it available?

At this point in my work with individual clients, someone will invariably get upset with me and say, "I don't like hearing about my ostrich. That's why I have it—to avoid looking at these problems." A reasonable statement. My response goes something like this:

You've found out a lot about yourself and are on the edge of discovering a lot more. That unknown has to be somewhat frightening. The ostrich doesn't like to have his head yanked from the sand, remember, and he'll fight you for a while until he sees that you're serious about this hunt.

Just knowing that the Ostrich Complex plays a major role in your life isn't enough. It's too complex to take on all at once, something akin to building a new house without thinking of it in terms of a foundation, a series of walls, ceiling, and a roof. The job can seem overwhelming unless we conceive of it in smaller, more easily managed parts.

That's what this chapter is all about. We're going to take your Ostrich Complex apart. We're going to do that through several mini-tests that I've written for you. They're short and not too imposing. I think you'll find them interesting in that they'll help you see more clearly where in your life *your* ostrich calls home.

Not seeing an ostrich in one part of your life doesn't mean there isn't one somewhere else. You may feel that you're ostrich-free on the job, but your ostrich may have settled in at home. If both work and home are clear, your ostrich may well have found refuge in your other personal relationships—perhaps in one particular one rather than in all of them. People are different, so, of course, your ostrich isn't going to behave just like everyone else's. Being able to distinguish among your ostrich's favorite hangouts—home, work, and interpersonal relationships— is essential to your understanding and growth.

Through these mini-tests, I'm going to ask you to divide your life into the three ostrich areas I've just mentioned. Of course, there's a certain amount of overlap; after all we work not just on the job but also at home. Interpersonal relationships are important all the time, whether with colleagues, family, or friends.

I've arranged the questions, therefore, into groups for each of these three areas. For the first two, I've subgrouped them into *routines* and *responsibilities* at work and at home. I'm asking you to consider each of these areas in light of your overall Ostrich Complex.

THE TWO R's: ROUTINES AND RESPONSIBILITIES

Does your ostrich arrive to keep you from the daily, basic routine tasks that you need to do? Prevent you from writing simple memos? Keep you from performing regularly scheduled activities? Or does it take over when there are significant responsibilities that you are involved with, blocking you from making personnel decisions or preventing you from asking for help when you need it? Ostriches make no distinction between small stresses and big ones; they apply their inappropriate coping methods to any challenge.

The Mini-Tests. I've found with my clients that it's important to know not only into which areas of your life the Ostrich Complex has moved, but also whether it "helps" you avoid routines or heavier responsibilities. Since such a division is important to our search for the ostrich, I've designed the following sections to examine work, home, and interpersonal relationships in terms of routines and responsibilities. Each mini-test contains statements that need a simple answer based on the scale that accompanies each one. The scoring is also very straightforward. I'll discuss the scoring process at the end of the first section.

That way you'll at least take the first test without knowing exactly what a "very little" or "very much" answer means. You'll be transferring all of your scores from these mini-tests to a summary sheet later in this chapter.

Here's your first mini-test. Choose the number that best represents how true each statement is for you, and put that number in the blank next to the statement.

THE WORLD OF WORK—RESPONSIBILITIES

1	2	3	4
Very Little Like Me	*A Little Like Me*	*Pretty Much Like Me*	*Very Much Like Me*

1. I am most productive when I work unsupervised. _____

2. I plan extra "just in case" time when working to meet a deadline. _____

3. When I don't understand a task I ask someone for help. _____

4. If a subordinate's work isn't up to my standards, I am able to confront the situation effectively. _____

5. If someone above me interferes with my work, I negotiate for a more independent situation. _____

Total Points   [_____]

HOW TO SCORE THE MINI-TESTS

Add up the number of points that you assigned to the five questions. That number is your score for this mini-test. Your score can range from five to twenty points for each one. A summary chart for all of these scores is on page 70. Transfer your score from this section, *Work—Responsibilities*, to the appropriate place in that chart.

How did you score? I'm sure that just from these five questions you've got an idea of how much ostriching you do when it comes to responsibilities at work. Did you answer "Very Little Like Me" to question 3 as Walter did? Did you assign a 1 to question 5 as Glenn did? Since the impact of each of these areas on your life is very personal, I don't have any stringent cutoffs for what scores constitute high, medium, or low. It's more important for you to compare this mini-test and its area of your life to the others. You'll do that with the summary chart in a short while. For now, let's see how your answers compare to Deirdre's.

Deirdre. How would our emotionally paralyzed but potentially brilliant lawyer score on the same questions? Productive when unsupervised? No. She was much more productive as a legal aide, when there was someone above her. Does she plan "just in case" time to help with deadlines? She used to in her old job, but not now. In fact, she finds it hard to make any plans now and hasn't been meeting any of her deadlines, either. Has she asked for help? No. Deirdre believes she *should* be capable of doing the work by herself. She knows how to do the work, she just can't bring herself to do it. Discussing the problems with any of her colleagues would force her to face what is happening more than she wants to. Deirdre has a large number of no answers in this section; there's obviously an ostrich well encamped in this part of Deirdre's life. That ostrich is making it difficult, if not impossible, for Deirdre to take necessary responsibilities at work.

On to the second mini-test for work. Remember to choose the number that best represents how true each statement is for you.

THE WORLD OF WORK—ROUTINES

1	2	3	4
Very Little Like Me	*A Little Like Me*	*Pretty Much Like Me*	*Very Much Like Me*

1. The material things I work with are easy to find when I start my day.   _____

2. I am able to start and finish work smoothly each day.   _____

3. It is easy for me to adapt my work habits to new equipment, procedures, and people.   _____

4. I arrive punctually in the morning and after lunch.   _____

5. It is easy for me to remember tasks that need regular attention.   _____

Total Points   [_____]

How does your ostrich affect your handling of routines at work? Do you let return calls and memos pile up, lose track of folders, and get in too late to plan your activities before the phone starts ringing? Such *little* things can lead to *big* stress. Are these areas ostrich territory for you? Remember to take your total score from this mini-test and transfer it to the summary chart on page 90.

Let's move our search into your home.

THE WORLD OF HOME—RESPONSIBILITIES

1	2	3	4
Very Little Like Me	*A Little Like Me*	*Pretty Much Like Me*	*Very Much Like Me*

1. I have some funds set aside so I can easily handle having to make un-expected repairs on the house. _____

2. I handle disagreements with neighbors easily and effectively as they arise. _____

3. I have a clear idea of the best possible place to move to in case I decide to move suddenly. _____

4. I deal effectively with the company involved when something is wrong with a product or service. _____

5. I find it easy to start new major projects at home without having them interfere with my family and work relationships. _____

Total Points [_____]

Julie and Ken. Let me tell you a little about Julie and Ken, another couple who've been to my office, so that you can compare your score here to how they would have answered these questions. They once sat in my office arguing about the furnace in their apartment house. It's in an old building, and the heating system hasn't been updated for years, so their unit stays a little chilly.

"*Ken,*" said Julie, clearly enough for him to know what was coming by that tone. "Have you been over to talk to Mr. Morgan about the heat?"

"Julie, it's an old furnace. There's not much he can do about it."

"Why don't we ask him to get a new one then? It's his responsibility, isn't it?"

"Just wear a sweater like I do, Julie. And move around some. You just sit in one place. No wonder you're cold. Remember, Morgan's place has the same problems ours does. I'm sure he'll fix it soon."

Have either Ken or Julie been over to talk with Mr. Morgan? No. Ken tells himself it would be a waste of time; he just wears several layers of clothes when he's home. Julie tells herself that she shouldn't do it since Ken said he would.

This is part of Julie and Ken's shared Ostrich Complex. It's complete with many of the complexities: *Procrastination*—"I'll get to it soon." *Denial*—"It's not that bad really"; "Mr. Morgan will do it when he can." And *collecting*—"Ken, you keep saying you'll take care of it"; "Julie, when will you stop nagging me about it?" Meanwhile the problem remains unresolved—simply because neither will confront Mr. Morgan about fixing the furnace or getting a new one. That home responsibility is a worry, but it's left untouched and buried in a shared Ostrich Complex.

Let's check your OQ when home routines are involved.

THE WORLD OF HOME—ROUTINES

1	2	3	4
Very Little Like Me	*A Little Like Me*	*Pretty Much Like Me*	*Very Much Like Me*

1. I find it easy to keep within my budget. _____

2. I can usually find things quickly when I need them. _____

3. I do my chores on a regular schedule. _____

4. I have planned times at home just for relaxing. _____

5. I keep enough food on hand for unexpected guests. _____

Total Points   [_____]

None of the people we've met thus far really has home routines as major ostrich problems. Since I find it easier to tell you what I mean, however, when I put the ideas in the context of some people with whom I've worked, let me give you a brief introduction to a few new friends who have an ostrich in their home routines.

Marie. Marie is a CPA with a very good reputation for unraveling bookkeeping nightmares. But away from work you would think that she has never seen a checkbook, much less a balance sheet. Marie yells at herself each month when she finds she's missed a payment and has had to pay interest on a charge card. At tax time, you'll find Marie begging last-minute help from one of her associates for her own taxes—all this while she's hard at work computing taxes for multimillion-dollar corporations.

Stan. Stan has been a highly respected surgeon for fifteen years. He seems so disciplined that his interns often crack jokes about how Stan must be the bionic doctor. But if any of his patients saw him trying to find his car keys or wallet in the morning, they'd get more than a second opinion. Stan's friends have called him a klutz on more than one occasion. It's not just a habit he's learned, as you'll see in just a minute. It's his ostrich acting up.

Lani. Lani has two kids and a husband. When they are away during the day, Lani does a lot of volunteer work in the community. She's considered a top-notch organizer and runs many major fund-raising projects. Most of her domestic work is successful, as well—with one exception. Meals are almost always late or completely forgotten. Her husband often has to drive the kids out for fast food because Lani hasn't found time to make dinner. When she starts an elaborate meal for company, she frequently discovers halfway through it that an essential ingredient can't be found in the kitchen. More than one of Lani's dinners have been abandoned before they ever saw the table.

All of these people are successful, competent adults in careers or endeavors outside their homes. But not one seems to be capable of using organizational skills at home.

What is happening with them?

Marie, the CPA, grew up in a family where her mathematical skills were discouraged because they were "unfeminine." Nevertheless, she pushed ahead in the field at school. She resisted her home pressure and showed her parents she could make practical use of her talents to earn a good living. But somehow the attitudes she had to contend with while a child at home lingered. She will not let them interfere with her competence at work, but at home she has doubts about who she really is. Those doubts cause enough stress for Marie to distance her public success while she is at home. Her ostrich firmly in place, Marie started bouncing checks and having trouble keeping track of her money, fulfilling her parents' prophecy and her own worst nightmares.

For Stan, being orderly and attentive to the minutiae of surgery is so essential that he associates the very act of being awake and organized with work. That stress has built up a lot of resentment in Stan toward his work. He feels as though he can't escape the need to be perfect; he can't make mistakes without disastrous results. Thinking about work demands is so stressful that he lets his ostrich take over after work, however, by refusing to organize everyday details. At home Stan forgets most everything.

Lani's ostrich is similar. For her, organization belongs to the real world—the world outside her household. Although she won't let herself realize it, she would rather be doing something more important than cooking dinner. She thirsts for something real to do, and simply can't think of meals as an activity with any significance. Although her volunteer work is okay, it's not as important as what her husband does, because it's voluntary. But Lani's feelings of frustration remain buried in the background. Instead of expressing them openly, she collects them and, as a result, forgets some of her routines, like preparing dinner.

A psychological truism suggests that to be happy we need to do work we enjoy and have close interpersonal relationships. We've talked about the ostrich lurking in your workplace. Let's now look for the ostrich who may be hiding in your dealings with others.

I'm giving you two separate columns for your answers, so that you can answer the questions for work *and* for home situations. We'll score the mini-test for both and check for any differences between the two areas.

THE WORLD OF INTERPERSONAL RELATIONSHIPS

1	2	3	4
Very Little Like Me	A Little Like Me	Pretty Much Like Me	Very Much Like Me

	AT WORK	AT HOME
1. Most of my long-term relationships are rewarding.	_____	_____
2. It is easy for me to meet people I like.	_____	_____
3. When my spouse or colleague gets angry with me, I can handle it effectively.	_____	_____

	AT WORK	AT HOME

4. If someone does something I feel is inappropriate or even wrong, I can intervene without being afraid of making a scene.   _____ _____

5. In group decision-making, I am clear with others about what I want.   _____ _____

6. If someone to whom I am close criticizes me unfairly, I can handle the confrontation effectively.   _____ _____

7. I keep in contact with old friends, distant relatives, and former colleagues.   _____ _____

8. I know how people will act around me even before I meet them.   _____ _____

9. If someone dislikes me, it's easy for me to understand why.   _____ _____

10. If I do something wrong, I can handle others' telling me how it made them feel.   _____ _____

Total Points [_____] [_____]

                    WORK   HOME

How to Score This Mini-Test. Remember that there is no "best" number of 1 or 4 answers. We can look at the difference between the ostriches in your work and home relationships, however. Which column had the lower score? Which column has questions that describe you the least? That's where your ostrich is likely to be hiding. And what do your scores for each say about how you deal with people you love versus those you work with every day? Also look at the totals in each column compared to your work and home scores on the other mini-tests. Remember: Copy these scores to the summary chart as you did with the others. Your scores are really a guide to how much of a problem the ostrich is in the area of your interpersonal relationships. Let's turn to some of the people we've met and see how the ostrich in their relationships compares to yours.

Nancy. You remember Nancy. She's the one whose Ostrich Complex is strongly linked with her interpersonal relationships, most specifically with the one with Nick, her husband. Relationships at work are relatively easy for her to handle. At home, however, in interacting with the single most important person to her, Nancy has become unsure of herself. She is aware that Nick is now dissatisfied with her and their relationship. But she has not dared to discover the source of her uneasiness, at least not in any way that will improve the situation. Unwilling to take the risks necessary to develop a mature relationship, Nancy is condemned to continue pretending to be part of a "perfect couple" with Nick, though they both sense that there's something terribly wrong.

Roy. Another classic situation where a personal life has been lessened by the ostrich. His primary long-term relationship with Shirley is unrewarding, though he fights admitting it. Roy is not willing to cut it off and try to meet someone new. Even more important, perhaps, is the fact that he fights even finding out from Shirley how she feels about him. Roy is a classic example of the old denial adage, "Don't ask—you may find out."

Bob. Then there's Bob, the fellow who owed you money and then disappeared from your life. The date he promised to pay you has come and gone. You haven't heard from him, and it appears you aren't going to. Both you and Bob are burying your heads rather than taking a hard, but necessary, look at your relationship.

Interpersonal relationships, whether at home or at work, are complex and convenient localities for the wily ostrich. It spreads a comforting sand blanket over our insecurities, as Walter's ostrich does in his relationship with his boss. It delays confrontations and lets us refuse to recognize our fears of being rejected by others, as Deirdre's ostrich does under the guise of pursuing perfection.

WHERE YOUR OSTRICH CALLS HOME— SUMMARIZED

Let's talk overview. You've taken five mini-tests designed to help pinpoint where in your life the ostrich calls home. If you haven't done so already, take those scores and transfer them to the Work, Home, Interpersonal Relationships Summary Chart.

WORK, HOME, INTERPERSONAL RELATIONSHIPS
SUMMARY CHART

	My Score	Possible Score
WORK—RESPONSIBILITIES	_____	20

This area *for me* is:
Not a problem ____ a small problem ____ a major problem ____

WORK—ROUTINES	_____	20

This area *for me* is:
Not a problem ____ a small problem ____ a major problem ____

HOME—RESPONSIBILITIES	_____	20

This area *for me* is:
Not a problem ____ a small problem ____ a major problem ____

HOME—ROUTINES	_____	20

This area *for me* is:
Not a problem ____ a small problem ____ a major problem ____

INTERPERSONAL RELATIONSHIPS—WORK		
	_____	40

This area *for me* is:
Not a problem ____ a small problem ____ a major problem ____

INTERPERSONAL RELATIONSHIPS—HOME		
	_____	40

This area *for me* is:
Not a problem ____ a small problem ____ a major problem ____

Overview. You have probably rated one or two specific areas as more of a problem for you than are the others. Those greater problem areas are the ones to concentrate on as we move into our discussion of the costs of the Ostrich Complex and how to change it. The Summary Chart will help you consider how your life would change if your ostrich were gone. You are already able to imagine some of those changes. Work will go more easily and be more enjoyable. Love relationships will be more satisfying and less frustrating. You will have more energy for the exciting parts of life when the little things that you now ostrich are handled more rationally.

The Ostrich Complex should be an unwelcome guest or tenant. That's true whether it lives with us at work, at home, or in our relationships with others. The Ostrich Complex is more like a squatter in our lives—and few of us can afford to let the ostrich occupy the same piece of territory long enough to get squatter's rights. It's possible to lose a large piece of your life, a loss none of us can afford. That's our next issue: What does the ostrich complex cost to keep around, and is it worth it?

Chapter 5

Costs of the Ostrich in Business and Personal Relationships

THE BUSINESS OF THE OSTRICH COMPLEX

One million workers call in sick on any given work day.[5] Many are sick from stress. In fact, the National Institute for Occupational Safety and Health conservatively sets the loss to companies just from "executive stress" at more than $20 billion each year. Add to that amount the cost of the 18 percent of work time lost each year because of employees who waste time—a form of employee procrastination—and the dollar cost is almost unimaginable.[6]

The causes of this tremendous waste are some of the basic symptoms of the Ostrich Complex: the inability to handle stress, difficulty in making decisions, lack of understanding about the job demands. How many of such workers do you know personally?

How many colleagues do you know who are like this client of mine? He won't complete expense account forms until they total quite a large sum. Meanwhile his company is earning interest on *his* money and he's losing interest on money that could be in his bank account because he hasn't gotten around to turning in a simple report. He, and others like him, say, "It's just too much trouble. I'll get to it soon." And how many times has the work ostrich reduced your efforts, efficiency, and money? If you're heading up the ladder of success, the ostrich can be your downfall.

The Ostrich Complex diminishes our abilities, drains our energies, and reduces our efficiency at work. Who needs one as a business partner? Is he one of yours? Did your mini-tests suggest that your ostrich has found a home in your business life? If so, this next material is essential for you. We'll also look at a similar cost analysis for the ostrich in your personal life. As you've seen, a fear of change, a reluctance to face problems head-on, is common in our personal life as well as our work life—and the two can and do overlap. I've found ostriches operating even in the things that I do for fun.

Here's one of them. I'm not a great tennis player, but I'm not too bad, either. I'd been playing for years with the same wooden racquet when it began to crack. Now, as most people know, everyone has been switching to aluminum or graphite racquets for their better weight distribution and power. My playing partners and opponents swear by the new designs and materials. They constantly offer to lend me one of their racquets or badger me about the problems I've been having with mine.

It's become a running joke among my friends that I spend more time scouring the country looking for someone to repair my "old wood" than I do playing tennis. The repair shops, too, tell me to dump the racquet and buy one of their new models. I've probably spent more money on phone calls and gasoline than it would have cost me to buy a new racquet. Sure, I shared in the humor—most of it. But for a long time I refused to buy a new racquet even though I was having to turn down a lot of enjoyable matches.

Was I ostriching by refusing to throw away my old racquet and move into the new age of tennis? Or was I just holding on to something I was comfortable with, that I liked to keep the same? You can tell the difference when you look at the costs of my refusing the change.

The search for a repair shop wasn't fun; in fact, it was expensive in terms of time and dollars. The missed opportunities to play and the frustrating arguments with my friends were not enjoyable, either. But my ostrich kept me from having to face my actual performance limitations. It gave me an excuse not to be as good as I wanted to be. It let me stay mediocre without accepting the fact that I performed at a lower level than I wanted to. My ostrich drained energy that I needed for other personal growth parts of my life that had nothing to do with tennis. Finally I did get a new racquet. Writing about the Ostrich Complex is an excellent way to have to face the fact that you're ostriching.

What does ostriching with my hobby have to do with the ostrich in business? Just imagine for a moment that instead of my being someone determined to stick with an old racquet, we're talking about the president of a U.S. automobile firm, who's determined to stick with manufacturing cars along the lines that were established years ago. He's denying the incursion of foreign competition, hiding from the need to rethink his methods and marketing. His company must adapt to new designs, manufacturing styles, and techniques because if they don't, they'll soon be out of business. The "tennis racquet attitude" prevailed in the U.S. auto industry during the late 1960s and early 1970s. It was during this period that American car makers continued to build giant gas guzzlers in spite of all the evidence that the American people wanted and needed smaller, more fuel-efficient cars that cost less. What happened? You probably remember the long lines at gas stations when fuel for those guzzlers was in short supply and how the American auto industry bordered on collapse because so many people were buying cars made overseas.

Lee Iacocca, formerly of Ford and the man many credit with saving Chrysler Corporation from bankruptcy, described Henry Ford's reaction to the oil crisis in this way: "He was worried about the OPEC situation. Convinced that a major depression was imminent, he ordered two billion dollars scratched from future product programs. With this decision, he summarily eliminated many of the products that would have made us competitive—such necessities as small cars and front-wheel-drive technology.

"I was furious. General Motors and Chrysler were working feverishly to bring out their subcompact. But the head of the Ford Motor Company had stuck his head in the sand."[7]

No one has yet come up with the actual cost for what it

took to feed the ostriches in Detroit, but estimates range into the hundreds of billions of dollars.

Decisions about things such as car sizes and styles have clear impact on the success or failure of a company. An Ostrich Complex that impedes that decision-making process is too costly to maintain. The costs of daily routine problems may seem less impressive in impact, but how many of them are there?

Daily problems, hassles in everyday routine activities, can be just as costly to a business. In fact, one of my first concerns when I begin consulting with a company is to gain an overview of their daily routines, from that of the stock boy to that of the chief executive officer. Why? I do it because one of the most fascinating things that psychologists have found to be true is the effects of daily hassles on business stress levels.

Two researchers in particular, Drs. Perry London and Charles Spielberger, found in their experiments that "the little problems do add up, taking more of a toll on health and well-being than the rare major crises."[8] That idea is even more important when we turn to the business executive who has been promoted to a new position. London and Perry found that for this group, "the petty details of their new positions—not the burden of added responsibility—were the chief causes of their troubles."[9]

I've noticed how much time companies will take to indoctrinate the new secretary to the daily details of *that* position. Those same companies then leave their new managers and vice-presidents to their own devices when it comes to uncovering how to handle *their* daily routines. The new executive, of course, often doesn't care to admit that he is bothered by the basics or that he/she is having trouble finding them out. The individual and the company waste meaningful time and energy. The daily hassles wind up being stressful for the individual. Such stress triggers the Ostrich Complex, and the ostriching then costs the company far more money than it realizes—or can afford.

Companies are geared to recognize the big stressors. When I ask CEOs for their views of what might be creating stress for their employees, I find they have no trouble identifying the *big* stress that's present or on the horizon. The proposed relocation to another city, a lower than expected quarterly report, renegotiation of a union contract are clearly identified stressors. As psychologist Richard Lazarus has pointed out, such stressors are big enough to stand out and be seen as challenges. For most of us challenges add zest to life. They're what make the corporate life-style so appealing; for many, *la raison d'être*.

Instead, it's the little problems that often sneak up on us, triggering an Ostrich Complex, draining our energies, nickel-and-diming us into a form of stagnation. As is characteristic of the ostrich, the little hassles surround us before we even have a chance to look up and get prepared. The size of the problem may not be nearly as important as the *number* of problems.

In addition to how employees respond to daily stress, there is also the issue of avoidable stress that is created by certain management approaches. Harvard psychologist Harry Levinson, for example, has identified the stress that is avoidable even in major stressors such as a corporate merger.[10] Though most people know that there will be reductions in the workforce of the acquired company, he points out that "most people want to hang on to the status quo. They keep hoping that they won't be the ones who are let go or have to pull up stakes.''[11] In essence, they deny that they will be the ones affected. The ostrich keeps telling them, ''Don't worry. It'll happen to someone else, not to you.''

What does happen? Levinson tells us how the results include the most common stress symptoms—headaches, backaches, depression, lethargy, and a decline in productivity. These show up in almost all of those worried about losing their jobs in a merger. Part of these symptoms, of course, are inevitable personal reactions to a frustrating situation.

A larger part of the symptoms, however, relate to a standard ostrich procedure in most companies. Particularly in the midst of mergers, management is often notorious for its head-in-the-sand approach to employees. The standard practice is to deny that there is a problem (too many workers) and then to allow rumors to cause the inevitable stress and damage, raising suspicions and stress levels, leading to a drop in the amount of real work done. Management can literally drive employees crazy with uncertainty, contradictory messages, and vague, threatening maneuvers. No one wins from sharing this ostrich among management and employees.

What should be done? To begin, employees faced with this kind of situation need to clarify what is happening to them. If they cannot do that as a group, then they must do it as individuals. It is important for them to make plans based on as informed an understanding of the company situation as each can get. At the same time, management must communicate as clearly as possible with *all* employees, especially those who are likely to be affected by the impending changes. All involved have to recognize the realities of the future so that realistic plans can be made.

In dealing with the Ostrich Complex in business, communication between management and employees is the key. A company's credibility with its employees depends on how clearly and how far in advance it communicates impending *bad news,* such as plant closures, layoffs, or pay cuts, to its workers. There is no better way to undermine the confidence of employees than by leading them to suspect that the management itself is refusing to face impending problems realistically. Once that happens, once the employees get the idea, even unconsciously, that management has its head buried in the sand, how much confidence can we expect workers to have in *anything* they are told?

If employees are not informed, how likely are they to believe that nothing is really going on? Not very likely. The proliferation of wild and contradictory rumors can do tremendous damage to already shaken morale, thus intensifying any other problems the company may have. Confidence drops among the employees and then spreads rapidly to the public.

The Continental Illinois Bank crisis of 1984 is a classic example of rumor bringing down the house. The Continental Illinois Bank of Chicago, seventh largest in the United States, was really no worse or better than any other large bank in the country when the rumor of losses began to spread among employees in the spring of 1984. Within days, rumors had become public and the run on the bank's reserves reached the point where bank officials had to call on the Federal Reserve and the FDIC to loan them emergency funds.

At the same time, however, public statements from the

bank's management kept insisting that everything was fine. A month after the first federal bailout, Continental Illinois was faced with an even larger drain on its resources as depositors continued to withdraw their funds. Only a massive bailout package and an unlimited guarantee of all deposits by the federal government ultimately saved one of the world's largest banks from going under.

The severity of the crisis was later blamed on the bank's management, which adopted a policy of saying that everything was under control, when it was obvious to employees and then the public that some things were not under control. The bank's real debts have been described as a less critical factor than the management's public posture of denying that there was any problem. It was a collective ostrich of mammoth proportions.

As I've seen in many companies, and as you've seen here with cars and money, ostriches can affect entire groups of otherwise competent and intelligent people just as easily as they affect each of us individually. The cost to such large corporations can be astronomical. It can be just as immense to you, however, and to the company for which you work.

Let's take another look at Deirdre, the attorney. Her ostrich may be making it easier for her to avoid having to confront her need to be perfect, but at what cost? Her ostrich is well on its way to costing her a hard-won career as an attorney, as well as her self-image as a competent adult. It's also expensive for her law firm.

Such is definitely the case for Walter and his company. He is obviously a valuable employee who has done a lot for his firm over the years. To give him Jessica without explaining whether she's to be his replacement because he is to be fired or promoted, is to give Walter an ambiguous if not lethal message. Worrying about that message impairs his productivity, damaging not only his morale, but that of his co-workers who see what has happened and can only speculate—and generate rumors—about the reasons. Isn't it logical to assume that they, too, will start feeling insecure about what management has in store for them? When that does happen, you can see that a chain of ostriching will have begun, started and fed by management's own Ostrich Complex.

Walter has certainly done his own share of ostriching about these issues, but so, apparently, has higher management. By not telling Walter what Jessica is being trained for, management is procrastinating or denying Walter's need to know and is harming him and the company.

It is not that Walter can't handle stress. His entire career and his personal life show that he handles it very well. He didn't get his "Ralph Nader Award" by shying away from stress and challenges. But the present fears are, he feels, out of his control, brought to the surface by Jessica's appearance in his work life. Is he really seeing smoke where there is no fire? Or is something shifty going on? Walter doesn't know because he's made no attempt to find out. He's so confused by the ambiguity of the situation and his own feelings of helplessness that he doesn't know what to do. On the other hand, no one above him has been straight with him either. Walter has been told nothing in a situation where it's quite normal for him to respond to a lack of information by becoming anxious. Someone above him is avoiding necessary action as well.

I've had executives tell me that their real reason for not telling employees what was going on was that they wanted to be helpful and kind. They didn't want to get the employees upset so they chose to say nothing—a parental model of business that almost always backfires, particularly when it's management's ostriched fear of confronting the employees that keeps them silent.

Psychologists used to do something similar in psychological experiments. Researchers would not reveal anything about the purpose of the research to the subjects, in that way supposedly preventing the subjects from modifying their usual behavior to adjust for what they thought was being examined. You can probably guess what happened. Subjects would generate their *own* ideas about what was being researched and change their behavior anyway to meet the imagined demand characteristics of the study. It seems that all of us generate ideas in the absence of ones that make sense in order to alleviate our own anxiety. Giving the subjects a general purpose of the study became a necessity in order to keep self-generated and erroneous ideas from ruining data collection.

My friend Glenn's ostrich is slightly different. He's not dealing with vagueness from superiors, but, rather, from too many contradictory tasks assigned to him in a way that generates self-doubt rather than a challenge to be met. We've already discussed whatever gains there are for Glenn, such as avoiding any immediate trouble with his boss, Mr. Stevens. The unfortunate situation for Glenn is that his own pain will have to get greater before he becomes willing to confront his ostrich.

Glenn's Ostrich Complex also has a partner, just as Walter's does. It is Mr. Stevens' management style, after all, that gives Glenn such a strong incentive to adopt and raise his own pet ostrich. That style is costly not only to

Stevens, himself, and Glenn, but also to others in the company. And the cost to the company is great. Glenn's relationship with his boss will make future cooperative efforts difficult. His immediate projects will suffer and his low morale and self-doubt will probably make his future performance less valuable than it could have been. Mr. Stevens gets his desired results immediately so that they seem rewarding to him. In the long run, however, his method will be ineffective in dealing with his staff. It's likely that other employees already know of his management style, and that morale and trust in his leadership will drop.

Sullen resentment and fear are not moods that make for efficient work on anyone's part. A manager who encourages such negative attitudes is simply cultivating inefficiency, no matter what other reasons he or she may have for doing so. Regardless of the other costs an Ostrich Complex may have, one cost is always paramount—efficiency. It doesn't matter if you measure efficiency in your company as money-over-time or as money-over-work, it's still money that is slipping away.

Now that you have an idea of where the ostrich is in your business, a major question probably remains: How can I measure the costs of the Ostrich Complex in my own business? In my own personal life? That's the purpose of the questions that follow, written for you to use in assessing the costs of your own ostrich. Answering them for your own personal situation will help you identify your company's own bottom line in terms of ostrich behavior costs. I give a similar list to my clients to put both on their desk and on their refrigerator to help them calculate the costs of their personal ostriches as well.

COST-ANALYSIS QUESTIONS

- If you didn't have to feed this ostrich, what would you be doing? What is your ostrich keeping you from doing? And what does that cost you—in time, money, efficiency, friendship, health, self-esteem?
- How does your Ostrich Complex protect you? What does it help you avoid? What is so dangerous about doing what you are avoiding?
- What does your Ostrich Complex give you in return for all the things you do for it? Do you actually get something out of it that you don't want to give up?
- What kind of pain does your Ostrich Complex cause? And how much? How much pain (or cost) will it take before you will be willing to take action and do something about it?

PERSONAL COSTS OF THE OSTRICH COMPLEX

Businesses keep track of income and expenses by recording what comes in and what goes out. From these accounts a balance sheet is drawn up. Such accounting can be done for a business, part of a business, even for a single piece of equipment. You can do it, too, for your own Ostrich Complex.

You've probably done it for other pets you may have considered owning. Remember that cute Great Dane puppy a friend offered you? You were tempted, but then you mentally made up a balance sheet to help with the decision. What are the benefits of owning that dog? Protection, companionship, exercise, and so on. And what are the liabilities? Cost, space, getting up at five to walk him, and so on. In the end, you tried to make up your mind based on what was best for you in that situation. If you decided you couldn't take the dog, you were no doubt disappointed but comfortable in that you had thought out the decision. If you took the puppy and really didn't want to, you are no doubt sitting there as you read this thinking, "Why did I?" Along with that puppy, you may also have picked up a pet ostrich to keep you company.

Think about the other little things that you do that could use a cost-analysis approach. Maybe it's the fact that you never finish one tube of toothpaste without opening another one. I have friends who leave so many tubes out without the caps that suddenly they get disgusted with the dirt in the caps, throw the bunch of tubes away—and open another one.

I know that toothpaste tubes aren't the most significant aspect of your life, but think about all the little things that you do that bug you—over and over—and what the costs are. Pick a few tasks that threaten to drive you crazy each day and apply accounting techniques to them. It may be the washer you were going to have fixed and didn't—so you've been going out to the laundromat for weeks. Or it may be the clanking in the rear end of the car. Or it may be the items you borrowed from a friend and just keep putting off returning, making it a little harder each day to face him. I think you'll find that though it's just a little expense each time, by the end of your cost accounting, the amount in time, money, and energy is quite large.

So what have we learned about corporations that can help us in our own lives? Let's look back at a few of the friends we've already met and see where they fit into such an analysis.

Marie. Her Ostrich Complex is firmly settled into the routine aspects of her personal household economy. She often loses control of her own finances, despite her wizardry with everyone else's. Does she get anything pleasurable out of forgetting to pay parking tickets until they've doubled or from bouncing personal checks? Nothing at all. Does Marie avoid anything with her ostrich behavior? Yes: She avoids dealing with her accumulated conflicts about her abilities, her family's attitudes, and her confusion about who she really is. As a result, she is unable to take complete control of her life or feel comfortable in dealing with anything that may come up.

What will induce Marie to change? She can clearly tabulate the mounting costs in dollars: the bounced check charges, the late payment interest on credit cards, and the extra fines on her parking tickets. The threat to her career as an accountant may be the cost that she is finally unwilling to pay. Serious doubts would be cast on her abilities if clients and colleagues were to find out that she had gotten into a routine of financial inefficiency in her personal life. Marie may not be able to afford keeping that ostrich much longer.

Ken and Julie. Ken and Julie take their shared ostrich out for its exercise each day. What exactly do they gain or lose by having it around? To be sure, they avoid personally having to confront their landlord about the heat. They also add to what they have collected about each other's weaknesses and bad habits. And they avoid having to confront any other issues that have come up between them but which are buried as part of their ostrich behavior.

Their costs may have to mount significantly before they are willing to force their shared ostrich into the bright light of day—it will probably have to be a cold winter day, at that. It may take the threat of illness, or some actual physical problems, before one of them is willing to look at the folly they share. Too many ailments, including the Ostrich Complex, can thrive in the cold and dark. Ken and Julie may have to learn the true meaning of the Italian saying, *Dove non viene il sole, viene il medico*—"The doctor visits where the sun doesn't." The danger, of course, is that even when one of them does confront the heating problem, neither will examine the style that caused it to become bigger than it ever needed to be. When you're ostriching in one area with someone important to you, look out. Ask yourself what else are you *not* sharing? What else are you afraid to examine?

REDUCING YOUR EXPENSES

Whether we're discussing Great Danes or ostriches, there's no such thing as a free pet—particularly an ostrich. As I've tried to show you, everyone's ostrich has its own price range. There do seem to be two major expense categories to watch out for.

One ostrich can take the form of a steady tax on our energies and resources, much like a leaky faucet. As with Ken and Julie's shared ostrich, the loss is never great, but it still is a steady drain, usually an unnecessary one.

The more you feed ostriches, the faster they grow, and

the more they demand or take. That's certainly the case with Deirdre's, and it looks like it's about ready to happen to Walter's. An ostrich can be a greedy and hazardous pet to keep around. It might just nibble away at a single part of your life, or it might eat the hand that feeds it, and then work its way up your arm until . . .

So compute the cost of your own Ostrich Complex. If you didn't have to maintain it, consider what else you could be doing in your business life or your personal life.

Without careful consideration, few of us can assess the *real* costs of our pets. Everyone's answers to cost-analysis questions will be slightly different. Each of us needs to determine the cost of keeping our own ostrich, and evaluate those costs against gains. Once you've computed the bottom line for your ostrich you'll be in an excellent position to decide if and when to set it—and yourself—free.

Chapter 6

To Thine Own Style Be True: The Ostrich Complex and Your Personality Style

Ostriches are creative creatures: No two are exactly alike. Each lives, moves, and develops in a very specific environment—the everyday life of its owner. No two owners are alike; neither are their ostriches.

You must deal with your own Ostrich Complex by formulating your unique personal prescription. Another person's approach to handling the Ostrich Complex will not necessarily work for you. No one method fits all situations any more than does using one technique to put out all fires. Sometimes throwing water on a fire is the way to put it out, but if you're up against a grease fire in your kitchen, that's the last thing you want to do.

Friends may tell us, "Sure, that's happened to me. Just do it the way I did it and things will be fine!" Their mistake is similar to an unintentional one I've found parents make in trying to help. "Stand up and fight that bully at school," they may tell their child. They forget that some kids aren't meant to be scrappers. Mom or Dad may wish their son would get out there and fight, but for him a different way of handling that particular bully might need to be developed. We forget how much difference personality style can make in choosing the most appropriate way to deal with a problem.

I must admit I've advocated my own successful methods to friends. I've acted similarly as a therapist, too, *before* I began my research into the Ostrich Complex and into how people with different personality styles raise and train their own ostriches. I think that telling you what I did wrong will show you how I learned the vital importance of getting an Ostrich Change Strategy to fit the ostrich and its owner.

THE GENERIC PRESCRIPTION PROBLEM: GARY

Gary is thirty-eight years old and in an upper-management position at a fast-growing engineering research company. By all accounts he is less than two years away from becoming a vice-president. The problem is that he has been "less than two years" away from that goal for over two years already. Gary had been passed over for promotion twice when he came to see me.

Gary is so shy that it sometimes can be painful to be around him. But Gary is also quite talented, and there's no question that he does his job well.

When he didn't get the promotion he was expecting, Gary fumed to himself and withdrew from contact with his superiors whenever possible. You can guess how his superiors reacted. Based on their observation of Gary's behavior, they felt that they had made the correct decision. Gary did not—and could not—see the relationship between his shyness and the difficulties he was having getting along with his superiors. When it came to taking a close look at his own personality style and the problems it was causing him at work, he buried his head and became an ostrich. He denied his own role in the promotion decisions and began to see his superiors as the sole cause of his frustration.

It doesn't take an expert to see that Gary was angry and didn't know how to handle it. One of his stated goals when he came to me for therapy was "To become more assertive and get what I want."

One of Gary's friends had already coached him on the importance of assertiveness, telling him that it was the last word in effective human relations. "Gary," his friend told him, "you've got to stop letting them walk all over you. Go in there and stand up for yourself. *Demand* that they treat you right. *I did it with my boss*—and, boy, did he shape up!"

As a psychologist I know that there's a fine, but very important, line between being assertive and being aggressive. The difference is particularly important when dealing in power situations with someone such as your boss. Knowing this, I still made a mistake with Gary. We worked a lot on his becoming assertive—after all, that was the reason he came in—but I did not pay enough attention to his unique personality style. If I had, I would have seen that Gary's style was linked with the relationships he'd built up with his superiors, and with the way he buried his problems. Gary was so enthusiastic about becoming capa-

ble of fighting for his rights that we moved too quickly—
and in the wrong direction.

One day, acting on his own, Gary went in to see his
immediate supervisor. As you can imagine, he demanded
justice and released a lot of anger at his boss, thinking it
was part of what one does when being assertive. He railed
against the unfair treatment he had endured and blamed his
boss for much of it. Needless to say, his outburst was met
with an even more powerful and scathing response. Gary
failed to gain any of the goals he had set out to attain by
being assertive. In fact, Gary was lucky that he kept his
job.

"I knew it wouldn't work," Gary told me when he
came back in to see me. I could see that he was fuming
inside—at me. But he was unable to express those feelings, however much I deserved to share the blame for what
had happened. He calmly explained that it was probably
better for him to keep his anger and his problems bottled
up inside. He had withdrawn to the extent that all he did
was hope that the problems at work, and his relationships
with his superiors, would take care of themselves.

Gary's experiences were a shock to my own sense of
self-esteem as well as to his. They did point out to me,
however, that the Ostrich Complex behaves very differently with different people. Gary helped me see that I needed
to develop techniques for helping people with varied personality styles free themselves of the Ostrich Complex.
More important, I saw why the "right" technique with the
"wrong" person leads immediately to bad results. If you
try to change and fail, you may wind up believing that
ostriching is the best tactic for you to use.

                                        TRUE   FALSE

11. I know that if I work hard and do
     a good job, I'll be recognized
     and promoted.   _____   _____

12. When there are several people in
     the room, I usually have to clear
     my throat or do something similar
     to get their attention.   _____   _____

13. I'm more comfortable following
     the lead of someone else than
     taking on the responsibility
     myself.   _____   _____

14. I like to play very active
     competitive sports.   _____   _____

15. By paying attention, planning
     carefully, and making the
     right moves you can usually get
     what you want.   _____   _____

16. When a loud, obnoxious person
     at a party keeps pestering me,
     I'll leave rather than confront him. _____   _____

17. Most of the times I've gotten a
     break, it's just blind luck.   _____   _____

18. It's easy for me to express an
     opinion that is very different from
     that of the person I'm talking to. _____   _____

19. I run into a lot of unpleasant
     people and don't understand why.   _____   _____

	TRUE	FALSE

20. I let people know that I'm not
pleased when they criticize me
about my work.   _____   _____

21. What I do at work doesn't seem
to make much difference when it
comes to what others think of me. _____   _____

22. When someone gives me an
unreasonable amount of work to
do, I let them know it in no
uncertain terms.   _____   _____

23. I feel that if I can get in with the
right group, I'll end up okay even
if I mess things up.   _____   _____

24. Even small nuisances like parking
tickets that are unwarranted need
to be dealt with quickly and
firmly.   _____   _____

25. Finding the right lover is easy if
you take action when you meet
someone you find attractive.   _____   _____

26. If someone else wants something
strongly, I'll let them have it to
avoid the hassle.   _____   _____

27. If I were to lose my job tomorrow,
I'm sure that I could find
another one soon.   _____   _____

TRUE   FALSE

28. If someone tries to tell me what
to do, I usually bristle and
often refuse.   _____   _____

29. I've never had the right job,
mainly because of circumstances
rather than something I've done. _____   _____

30. I have more fun in relationships
when someone seduces me.   _____   _____

31. I can trace almost all of the things
that have gone wrong in my life
directly to things that I've done. _____   _____

32. I don't wait too long before asking
for the service I deserve when
I'm in restaurants or stores.   _____   _____

HOW TO SCORE THE PROFILE

The Ostrich Complex Personality Profile yields two separate scores, one for a personality concept that we in
psychology call "Locus of Control" (or, who or what runs
your life?); the other for the personality dimension of
"Aggressiveness-Passivity" (or, how forcefully do you
respond in situations?). To find your score for each section, compare your answers to those in the Answer Key.
Each time your answer matches the corresponding one in
the Key, give youself one point. Then transfer your scores
for the two parts to the Profile Graph that follows the Key.

OSTRICH COMPLEX PERSONALITY PROFILE

ANSWER KEY

Note that the scales alternate questions from the test; for example, Question 1 is on the Locus of Control Scale while Question 2 is on the Aggressiveness-Passivity Scale; thus the odd-numbered questions equal the Locus of Control Scale and the even-numbered form the Aggressiveness-Passivity Scale.

LOCUS OF CONTROL		AGGRESSIVENESS— PASSIVITY	
1.	F	2.	T
3.	F	4.	F
5.	T	6.	T
7.	F	8.	F
9.	T	10.	T
11.	T	12.	F
13.	F	14.	T
15.	T	16.	F
17.	F	18.	T
19.	F	20.	T
21.	F	22.	T
23.	F	24.	T

LOCUS OF CONTROL	AGGRESSIVENESS— PASSIVITY
25. T	26. F
27. T	28. T
29. F	30. F
31. T	32. T
[ ] ....TOTAL SCORE........ [ ]	

OSTRICH COMPLEX PROFILE GRAPH

Transfer your scores from the Locus of Control and Aggressiveness parts of the test to the Graph by circling the appropriate scores on the profile. Unless your scores are both 8, you will find that your scores place you into one of the four personality types on the Graph. A detailed discussion of each one comes a little later. Some brief descriptive phrases are presented here to give you an idea of what your scores mean in terms of your ostrich.

(Extreme sense
Internal Locus

16*

Feels in control of events but prefers to be left alone by others; low anger but finds that a strong superior or strict organization is frustrating

Control of own life and events is important; responds with selective anger to frustration by others

15*

14*

13*

———— TYPE I-P ———— 12*

11*

Uncomfortable around open expression of anger by others or in venting own feelings of frustration; feels in control but gives in to others to avoid conflict

Calm approach to most situations although feelings of helplessness are frequent and can produce anger

10*

9*

P
A
S
S
I
V
E

8——

0 1 2 3 4 5 6 7

8——

7*

Operates primarily to avoid conflict; high need to avoid situations that may produce anger

Wait-and-see attitude toward taking control in most situations; likely to be seen as reserved but known to show anger when very frustrated

6*

5*

———— TYPE E-P ———— 4*

3*

Pervasive attempt to go along in order to get along; most comfortable in high-structured jobs and relationships; avoids anger and conflict at all costs; feels helpless to deal with either

Finds it difficult to understand why things go wrong except that someone else is responsible; frustration from helpless feelings likely to flare up in anger behavior

2*

1*

0*

External Locus
(Extreme feeling

of control)
of Control

*16

*15   Feels in control of what happens but responds selectively with hostile behavior when things go wrong   Feels responsible for almost everything that happens; feels angry at self and others when things go wrong; can easily alienate others with high level of anger

*14

*13

*12 ——————— **TYPE I-A** ———————

*11

*10   Feels generally in control of what happens and can respond selectively with strong emotions when warranted by events   Often expresses a high level of anger and then worries about own lack of control over situation and own emotions

*9

\- -8- -
       9   10   11   12   13   14   15   16
\- -8- -

A
G
G
R
E
S
S
I
V
E

*7   Feelings of control vary widely depending on situation; lack of control likely to be frustrating but not likely to produce high anger behavior   Anger at others and self frequently felt and probably expressed when frustration at lack of control in situation builds up

*6

*5

*4 ——————— **TYPE E-A** ———————

*3

*2   Frequent out-of-control feelings make it hard to see why things go wrong and then deal with them effectively   Feels put upon by others; worries about what others or uncontrolled events will do to cause pain; responds to frustration with high level of anger

*1

*0

of Control
of helplessness)

INTERPRETING YOUR SCORE: THE TWO PERSONALITY DIMENSIONS

As you can see in the diagram on which you plotted your scores, there are basically two extremes for each of the scales. You can score anywhere along each dimension. When we consider your two scores together, however, they characterize you as one of four personality types. Where you are on one continuum doesn't affect where you are on the other, meaning that the two dimensions are by and large *independent* of each other. But it is important that you look at how one affects the other as you deal with your ostrich problems.

Let's now look at what the dimensions are and what the poles mean.

AGGRESSIVENESS-PASSIVITY

Someone who is always ready to go, who likes challenges, who likes to get ahead of others, and who prefers situations in which he or she can win will score pretty close to the *Aggressive* pole. Alan, our anxious salesman from Chapter Two, has a style that put his score here. Alan rebelled against his parents' desire that he become a corporate lawyer. He chose sales instead and then spent much of his life trying to be perfect in order to show them that he was right.

On the other hand, someone who consistently retreats from conflict, or even from recognizing that there is a conflict, is near the other end of the scale—close to the *Passive* pole. Our ineffective suitor Roy is a person who approaches conflicts this way, especially in his relationship with Shirley.

LOCUS OF CONTROL

The other scale is more subtle. This dimension reflects how you think about your life in terms of control. Where you are on the scale shows how you react to the question "Who (or what) is in charge in your life?" I'm dividing this personality trait into two sections. Each one deals with the meaning of extreme scores, both high and low, on the Locus of Control scale.

External Locus of Control (Low Scores). People who feel that no matter what they do about a particular problem the outcome will be determined by someone else feel that the control over their lives lies *outside* their own control. They feel that there isn't much they can do about negative experiences, and that these are brought on by other people, their environment, or just bad luck. They are the people who read the horoscope each morning and then assume that's the way life will be regardless of what they do about it. Life for them, they feel, would be much better if only circumstances were different. Psychologists term this viewpoint an *external locus of control*. When I see people in therapy who feel this way about life, they tell me things such as, "No matter what I do, things don't get any better"; "I feel so helpless"; and, in extreme situations, "Life seems hopeless."

Internal Locus of Control (High Scores). Gary, our engineer, on the other hand, goes almost to the opposite extreme. Gary sees the problems he's been having as basically under his control, at times, almost too much so. He gets to the point where no matter what happens, he sees it as relating to something that he's done. *Internal locus of control* people tend to take the initiative in everything from job-related activities to relationships and sex. It's usually frustrating for them to sit back and let others take care of them. That same characteristic often prevents people such as Gary from seeking professional help. They are prone to statements such as, "I got myself into this, I can get myself out of it"; "I don't want someone else taking care of me"; and, for those in extreme situations, "It's all my fault."

THE OSTRICH AND PERSONALITY

Your personal degrees of locus of control and aggressiveness produce a unique environment for the Ostrich Complex that affects both the development of your Ostrich Complex as well as the best methods for you to rid yourself of it. Let's look at some of the ways these two personality dimensions interact with the ostrich and discuss some people we've met thus far in terms of these characteristics. Our discussion will follow the format of the Graph with a separate section that covers each of the four personality types and one for scores near the center.

Personality Type I-A: *"I'll* do it—or else!" If you've scored high on both scales, you see yourself as being responsible for almost all of what happens to you, taking your role in any situation very seriously. Consequently, when things go wrong, you are likely to blame yourself. Your high aggressiveness score suggests that you strike out when those things do go wrong, often at yourself, punishing yourself for what you perceive as your own inadequacies. Your ostrich finds this a useful tendency, getting you to flail away at yourself while the real problem remains neglected and unresolved.

This self-oriented aggression, while useful as a goad to self-discipline, can become a major obstacle to dealing effectively with ostriched problems. Since you see so much as under your control, it would be easy for you to develop a perfectionistic view of life—yours and others. Though you do well in independent situations, having to depend on others may cause you definitely uncomfortable, even anxious feelings. Worrying about doing and staying on top of everything creates an excellent breeding ground for the ostrich.

Somewhat lower aggressiveness scores suggest that although you feel responsible for most of what goes on in your life, you are likely to respond selectively to certain situations with an aggressive response. Perhaps you are more aggressive in family situations than at work, where you are a follower and not a leader. Moving from a situation in which you are in clear control to one where you have to depend on another may generate enough anxiety to bring out an aggressive response one time and a passive response another. Protecting your *sense* of self-control is so important and losing control produces so much anxiety that you are likely to deny that problems exist.

Type I-A: Walter. Walter is a fighter for social and consumer issues, yet he is having severe problems fighting in his own behalf. He has a definite sense that he *has* been in control of his own life, and he knows that he is usually very assertive. Though Walter's sense of control is firmly rooted in himself, he is now unable to deal with a situation that has somehow escaped him. What confuses Walter is that he has been thrown off balance by a *shift* in his *perception* of control—a very sudden shift at that. The shift in control has been brought about by Jessica's appearance as his trainee since it came at a time in his personal life where self-doubts about his career promise were beginning to creep in.

Walter was primed for the Ostrich Complex because he was already afraid of losing what he had achieved when an external threat, Jessica, mysteriously appeared. Walter has no clear sense of what is best to do or where the control for that part of his life now lies. Is it something he's done? Or is this problem the fault of a superior who doesn't understand what is best for the company? Instead of acting, Walter is retreating into the sand. In essence, he is blaming himself for not being in control as he assumes he should be.

Personality Type E-A: "*I* want *you* to do it—or else!" If both scores are near their respective extremes, most of what happens to you probably feels as though it is brought on by outside circumstances or by other people. As a result you expend a great deal of energy worrying about what others, or the situation, will do *to* you. If you read the newspaper and feel helpless about the world, your ire gets raised. You probably find yourself saying, "How could they do that!" That's your aggression talking.

You feel helpless to change things and angry at having to be that way. Your ostrich has you boxed in. If you consider making active changes in your life, you feel almost certain they won't work—you've probably been burned those few times you risked making changes. But frustration is the byword of your daily life. One danger is that you can lash out at those people and things that frustrate you, seeing them as more proof that you have no control over life: "They made me get angry." It's a vicious circle that says "Welcome" to the Ostrich Complex. At home you may be in the midst of a financial crisis but be transferring your anxiety into anger at the kids instead of planning to meet the crunch. The same pattern at work often manifests itself when managers direct more attention to employees' dress and manners than to dealing with major problems.

A medium aggressiveness score paired with a high locus of control score suggests that you feel that control over your life is located outside of you, but your response to those feelings varies. If you are supported, you can be very energetic. In another situation, however, you may act completely uninspired. When there are problems, you often choose to lie low and move out of the way, doing just what you are told—after all, you feel things won't change regardless of what you do. (That's your ostrich speaking!) Occasionally, however, you struggle, sometimes constructively, other times destructively, with the frustration you feel. Either way you gain or lose little personally since you react to the situation and are not motivated by any sense of trying to make a difference. It's hard for you to understand why you get criticized for acting inconsistent since your behaviors are merely responses to given situations. If you do get unhappy, your aggressiveness is likely to come out in indirect ways, such as procrastination or collecting. When "pushed" by the situation you can blow up, reduce your anger momentarily, and feel blameless. While you hide from the real problem, it remains to grow and cause you future frustration.

Type E-A: Deirdre. A motivated and generally aggressive person, she too now finds trouble because of a shift in how she perceives the control in her life. Deirdre functioned well as long as she saw the control as external. She is now paralyzed by having been put in almost total control of what happens to her. Is she failing at her new job so that she can put the control back into someone else's hands? Is she trying to convince herself that the decision to move to another job really was someone else's idea? People are often so uncomfortable at having control of their own lives thrust upon them that they'll work very hard to give the control back, even if it takes failure to do so.

This process forms an underlying theme in the lives of so many promising underachievers, people who sacrifice themselves, not to their careers, but to the ostrich.

Personality Type E-P: "*You* decide; I don't care." Roy's relationship with Shirley is a good representation of this situation. If you are this personality type, you probably don't feel in control of your life very often and you try to adjust to what others want as much as you can. Unlike Roy's case, however, your Ostrich Complex is active not just in dealing with other people; it's pervasive. It's a style of life that leads you to accept jobs where there are clear, almost automatic, guidelines and personnel policies. Such situations cater to your ostrich, because you can bury anything that may cause you anxiety. Being asked to take control of a project, however, will lead to procrastination; being angered by a boss or colleague will lead to collected feelings of anger. Your ostriching takes the form of surrendering completely to the program so that neither work nor others will place demands upon you.

Medium locus of control/low aggressive people approach the world on a pretty even keel but set as one of their primary goals the avoidance of conflict. For you this means that it can become almost automatic to bury your head because conflict avoidance is so important in your life. You may try to deny the real issue, as Ken and Julie did when arguing over the landlord, or try to avoid the problem altogether as Walter did. In either case, your low level of aggressiveness may not be a blessing when it allows the rest of the world to ignore your needs and wishes.

Type E-P: Glenn. Glenn is not very aggressive. Although he is motivated to get his work done well, he is passive when it comes to dealing with his boss. His passive attitude leads to his collecting behavior when Stevens (or most others) does something that angers him. With his external locus of control, Glenn also sees himself as merely responding to, and struggling to cope with, situations that from the start are defined and controlled by others. Glenn's ostrich enjoys this environment and will do little to help change matters.

Personality Type I-P: "I want to do it; but I don't mind if you do it." You see events in your life as indeed under your control, although you do not like to be in charge. This suggests that you are likely to seek an organized framework to help shape your activities, either in the form of regulations, as a powerful superior, or as another managing type of personality. Since you are good at following directions, when things go awry you feel they did so because *you* did not follow through well enough. Your search for something or someone to provide a structure for you provides a comfortable home for the ostrich. With your head buried, you can continue to find yourself at fault without ever having to examine what really is going on.

Type I-P: Margaret. Like Glenn, Margaret is also in a position of having bottled up something that needs to be taken to her boss. She is concerned about the inequality of her salary with that of her colleagues at work. She also is not very aggressive. Margaret is aware, however, that it is her own anxiety that is keeping her from addressing the salary inequities. Although passive, she has an internal locus of control. She sees herself as being responsible for what has gone wrong, but has great difficulty dealing with her anger appropriately. Margaret's anger gets ostriched as soon as it peeks from the sand.

Center scores: So you think you're average? This is the most fluid of all of the personality patterns and, because of that, potentially the most adaptable. If you find yourself here, you also found statements true for you within the other profile descriptions. On the positive side, you are less likely to have extreme responses than are those in the other groups. The bad news, however, is that you also have to deal more often with ambivalent responses to people and situations. You may at times not even be sure of what your response is—maybe you'd just as soon make no response. These unfocused feelings and this complexity make you a ripe target for any ostrich in search of a home. You can get so involved trying to figure out how you should feel and react that the anxiety that allows the ostrich to visit comes directly from those confused thoughts. You may at times wish you were more aggressive or more in control and bury your head to avoid examining your perceived deficiencies. The danger is that it's comfortable for you to slip back into old habits and patterns rather than continue with a new but riskier behavior. How many times have you seen a child who after learning a new skill apparently forgets everything he has just learned? After we have learned a new behavior, the anxiety of actually having to use it makes it easier—sometimes—just to go back to our old ways.

Center scores: Nancy and Nick. The relationship and the personality characteristics that distinguish Nancy and Nick are far less one-sided than they are for people with more extreme scores on these personality scales. In fact, theirs are surprisingly symmetrical. Nancy feels that Nick is in control, while Nick feels that control is vested in Nancy. Neither is willing to take real control and make changes. They are submissive, not to each other, but rather to the *image* they have of their perfect relationship and to their fear of evaluating that relationship. Any attempt to drag the problem into the open, even an attempt to admit that there is a problem between them, would feel like an attack on the relationship and on their shared ostrich.

Center scores: To control or not to control. It doesn't take long to realize, of course, that no one ever is, or ever can be, completely in control of his or her own life. I've had clients who have made that the goal of therapy only to find out that being in total control of their lives is impossible—and not eventually desirable. It is important, however, to understand that being largely in control means accepting responsibility for much of the good *and* the bad, for much of what goes right *and* for a lot of what goes wrong.

It is also rare for anyone to have completely lost control of everything, though during low times in your life you may feel that way. I mentioned earlier that clients will sometimes use the words "helpless" and "hopeless" to describe how they feel about life. Those words reflect the exaggerated *perception* that life is beyond their control. Some painful blow probably initiated these feelings, but, by and large, these people are looking through a tunnel at life and seeing only their lack of control in regard to the person or the incident that has hurt them. They forget all the aspects of life that still remain in their control and choose not to look at the choices they have in dealing with the cause of their Ostrich Complex.

And what now? Most of us have a lot in common with the center range pattern, so if you find yourself near the mid-ranges, you've got lots of company. But the purpose of the questions and discussion is to help you get a handle on your *own* ostrich and your *own* personality.

You've covered a lot of ground to this point, identifying problems that are complex even for professionals to understand. So it's important to stop for a moment and summarize where you started and where you see yourself now in terms of your Ostrich Complex. That summary is the goal and format of the next chapter.

Chapter 7

Your Ostrich Complex Summary

It's that time. Time to sit back and take stock of where you are in understanding and making decisions about your Ostrich Complex. I'm asking you to do for yourself what I do for others in my clinical practice.

I'm one of those clinicians who is always after his clients to evaluate how they're spending their time and money working on their problems. I think that it stems from my overall consumer orientation; I'm a lot like Walter in that regard. I find it ineffective—almost unprofessional—to have clients enter and continue therapy without setting aside specific times so that we can evaluate where we've been and where we're going.

Let's stop and do that kind of evaluation now.

Thus far, you've computed your score for the Ostrich

Complex Inventory and examined work, home, and interpersonal relationships to discover where your ostrich calls
home. And you've assessed your own personality profile
and considered what role your personality plays in your
Ostrich Complex. Here we bring it all together.

I have a caution for you before we begin. I'd like to
pass it on to you in the form of a story that I tell students
in my courses. Let's say that you are visited by a friend
who has a very bad habit of blinking his eyes. It seems he
never stops blinking. He tells you that it makes everyone
around him so nervous that they refuse to be in the same
room with him. "Tough to have lasting relationships that
way," he points out. So he has come over to see you for
advice. You can guess what happens. The blinking bothers
you to the point where you finally ask him, "How do you
expect me to help you when you sit there and drive me
crazy with that blinking. The sooner you stop that, the
sooner we'll be able to talk about what's bothering you."
Similar binds handicap clients in therapy unless the therapist is ready—and able—to deal with them.

Walter's situation is an excellent example. If you remember, Walter was in a general state of panic and felt
depressed about his future with the company. One of his
additional problems, however, was that he couldn't sort
out exactly what was needed in order for him to make
changes in his life. The ostrich doesn't pull his head out
easily, remember, particularly when its owner feels out of
control with regard to handling major life problems. Walter's
paradox, all too common in the Ostrich Complex, was that
the very problems he needed to examine were keeping him
from examining those problems.

I'd ask him to look at what was bothering him, and he'd

respond by getting even more nervous and upset. Thinking about the main problem in his life made him too anxious to examine it. I reminded him of the Ostrich Complex truism: *Ostriches don't like to have their heads yanked from the security of the sand.* Then we sat down and spent some time discussing the way he acted and felt in specific situations. Together we filled out some charts very similar to those that you've been using in this book. The result was that Walter started to feel he had a better chance of dealing with the stress and more control over what had seemed overwhelming. My bedside manner didn't by itself help him feel more in control. What did the job was that we divided the stress he was feeling into more easily managed bits, each of which was not overwhelming to him.

You'll find that this will be a brief chapter for you. Don't let the brevity fool you, however. What you're doing here leads directly to the next step, that of deciding what you want to change and then how to go about achieving those changes.

The following sections are a combination of a summary sheet and an Ostrich Complex report card. Complete them, giving yourself a grade for the appropriate areas by using the following grading scale. It's similar to what you remember from school. Remember that how you grade yourself is really up to you. You may score very few points on the Inventory, for example, yet find those few areas quite bothersome, even painful. Or, alternatively, it's possible that you could have checked many problems in an area such as Home—Routines, yet not really be much bothered by them and, consequently, give yourself a high grade. The grading is completely up to you. Like the other tests and charts you've used, its purpose is *your* self-analysis. It can be for your eyes only.

GRADING SCALE FOR THE OSTRICH COMPLEX SUMMARY

A+ Fantastic. Couldn't be better.

A Excellent. Overall, I'm quite pleased.

B+ Very good. But I can see a few minor aspects that need work.

B Good. There are some parts that cause me trouble.

C So-So. I make it through, but I do run into some sizable problems.

D Pretty bad. Some large-scale problems often get me down.

F Very bad. Couldn't be too much worse.

OSTRICH COMPLEX SUMMARY date _____

I. OSTRICH COMPLEX INVENTORY

Take your score from the Ostrich Complex Inventory on page 62 and write it here. Then evaluate how you feel about your own level of Ostrich Complex behavior using the grading scale.

score _____ grade _____

Take each of the scores for specific Ostrich Complex

behaviors from page 62, write them here, and then grade them using the same grading scale.

Perfectionism   score _____   grade _____

Denial   score _____   grade _____

Collecting   score _____   grade _____

Procrastination   score _____   grade _____

II. OSTRICH AT WORK—ROUTINES

Get your score for Work—Routines from page 90. Write it here and then evaluate your ostriching for routine activities at work. As a reminder, I've listed some of the aspects of Work—Routines that can be troublesome.

score _____   grade _____

Reminders:
- returning telephone calls
- handling daily paper shuffling
- meeting usual expected deadlines

III. OSTRICH AT WORK—RESPONSIBILITIES

Follow the same procedure here. Find your score on page 90, write it here and then grade your performance. Again, I've listed some potentially troublesome tasks for you to use as a guide.

score _____   grade _____

Reminders:
- providing feedback to those I supervise
- meeting unexpected deadlines
- using effective decision-making techniques

IV. OSTRICH AT HOME—ROUTINES

A similar task faces you here for Home—Routines. Your score is on page 90. Then grade yourself in this area of your life.

score _____   grade _____

Reminders:
- meeting daily expected demands
- keeping track of personal belongings
- cleaning up basic living areas

V. OSTRICH AT HOME—RESPONSIBILITIES

You'll find your score for this area on page 90. Copy it below and then grade your performance in this area.

score _____   grade _____

Reminders:
- bill-paying to avoid late charges
- handling repairs effectively
- planning major events

VI. OSTRICH IN INTERPERSONAL RELATIONSHIPS

Again for this area, copy your scores from page 90 and then describe how you do in dealing with interpersonal relationships using the grading scale.

WORK score _____   grade _____
HOME score _____   grade _____

Reminders:
* handling criticism from others
* dealing with feelings toward others
* problem-solving with work colleagues and/or family and friends

VII. OSTRICH PERSONALITY PROFILE

This section is somewhat different from those you've just completed. In addition to asking you to copy your scores on the personality profile to this page, I'm also giving you some statements to complete. This sentence completion task is one of the main ways we in psychology ask people to think about certain aspects of themselves.

Locus of Control Scale: Score _____
My score on this scale is in the (check one):
External direction   _____
Middle area   _____
Internal direction   _____

Now write a few words to complete these statements:

I feel most in control in situations where: _____

_____

I feel most out of control in situations where: _____

_____

When I do feel out of control I ostrich problems by:

_____

Aggressiveness Scale: Score _____
My score on this scale is in the (check one):
    Passive direction   _____
    Middle area   _____
    Aggressive direction   _____

Write a few words to complete these statements as well:

    I feel most aggressive in situations where: _____

_____

    I feel most passive or submissive in situations where:

_____

My (aggressive tendencies) (passive tendencies) cause me to ostrich problems when:

_____

_____

VIII. OSTRICH OVERVIEW

This next and final section is quite straightforward, but it represents your summary of all that you've listed here.

Consider its request carefully. Think about what your ostriched problems cost you each day. How would your life change for the better if the problems you are going to list here vanished? How will you feel if they remain?

The three ostriched problems that I most want to change are:

1. _____

2. _____

3. _____

Summary summary. No one else can make a judgment on what you have written in these sections or on what you have listed as the three ostrich problems that you most want to change. This summary is as individual as are the ways in which we live our lives. I know that completing it was not easy, but it was an opportunity for you to pull together a lot of your thoughts up to this point in the book. Our next major discussion focuses on setting the ostrich free. Your energies in completing this summary—in fact, in all that you've done so far—will be rewarded even more in the next few pages.

PART THREE

Setting Your Ostrich Complex Free

Chapter 8

Time to Be Ostrich-Free?

"I'm desperate," said Deirdre on her first visit to my office. "I saw an article in the paper about your work and realized that you were talking about *my* problem when you mentioned ostriching things that make us anxious."

Deirdre clutched a new briefcase in her lap with both hands as she told me about her inability to get her work done in a job apparently as new as her briefcase.

"It's too late, isn't it? I mean, don't you think I should just turn in my resignation and go back to my old job as a legal aide?"

"Did you come in hoping for a quick agreement with that decision?" I asked.

Deirdre shook her head. "That isn't what I want," she answered, a look of fright crossing her face. "But if you can't help me get on top of this thing . . . You can't work magic, and I don't have much time left. I haven't even really started on the work I've got to do yet, and the deadline is just a few days from now.''

"You're right. I can't work magic, but perhaps you can.''

"What do you mean?'' Deirdre asked me.

"Tell me, how does the thought of going back to your old job after failing with your first legal cases on this job make you feel?''

"Like I'm suffocating,'' she answered.

"Now tell me: Which feels worse, a really big failure, or a mediocre success?''

Deirdre shifted in her chair. After a long pause she said, "Most of the time it's really hard for me to see the difference between doing a mediocre job and a total foul-up.''

"But there is a difference?'' I asked.

"Well,'' she admitted grudgingly, "I guess there is.''

That statement was Deirdre's first step toward recognizing how fear immobilized her and how she used ostrich behavior to hide from that fear.

You may ask, "Wasn't Deirdre's first step when she contacted me for help and came into my office?''

It may seem so, but actually Deirdre was still under the protection and guidance of her ostrich when she first came in to see me. Her motive was to get my permission *not to do anything* about her problem. Deirdre's ostrich was feeding on her desperation and coming to see me was part of that desperation. In consulting me, Deirdre was choosing to talk about her work difficulties to someone *other* than the people at her law firm. Talking to me wound up helping, but a desire to release tension to people other than those directly involved is one of the ostrich's nasty traits.

We caught Deirdre's ostrich. In many ostrich situations, however, all of the initial corrective options we come up with are affected by the ostrich behavior itself. The long-range goal is to dump the ostrich completely; but it cannot be the first step. Trying too hard and too fast to be ostrich-free will throw the ostrich into a panic, setting off all sorts of alarms and additional ostrich behaviors. A disturbed ostrich kicks up a lot of dust. We can't yank it from the sand; we must ease it out.

The first step then is to see the problem—and decide to do something about it.

Deirdre Analyzed. Let's examine Deirdre's problem, analyzing it as though she were asking us why it exists and what she could do about it. Once we "see" her problem, understanding yours will be much easier.

Answer these questions from what you know about Deirdre. Look back over the information about her in the first few pages of this chapter and use that to fill in the blanks next to each question.

a. What am I (Deirdre) afraid of? _____

_____

b. How am I (Deirdre) dealing with my problem? ____

_____

c. What would be the easy way out? _____

_____

d. What do I (Deirdre) *really* need to do? _____

_____

How did you complete these questions for Deirdre and her ostrich problem? I'll give you my thoughts so you can see how well we agree.

a. Afraid of not being perfect; can't see the difference between a mediocre job and a total failure.
b. Dealing with fear by not even starting work.
c. Easy way out is to let boss fire her so she can return to safety of old job.
d. Really needs to look at why she's afraid to be less than perfect and deal with stress of having high level of job responsibility.

How did we do? Even if we disagreed, I hope you can see which information about Deirdre I used as a basis for my answers. What about your own answers to these questions? What are you afraid of? How are you dealing with it? What is the easy way out for you? What do *you* really need to do? Think about your answers to these questions. How would Ken and Julie answer them? Or Walter? Use the questions as a guide as you read more about some of the other people we've discussed.

PAIN, OR...MORE PAIN

Why is the Ostrich Complex so difficult to get rid of? Why are people so reluctant to change an unpleasant ostrich-induced behavior pattern? The answer is that we are afraid of the *unknown* future that change may bring.

Changing a habit, even one that causes us no end of discomfort and misery, is often more frightening than the pain we are experiencing *now*. People stay in unhappy situations, be they work, home, or relationships, not because they want to, but rather because they fear the *unfamiliar* experience and feelings that come with change.

All of us are attached to our tried-and-true routines and are loath to give them up, even when the routines are maintained solely to support a selfish and demanding ostrich. A fear of change is natural, but it can lead to unnecessary misery. What, then, induces us to take the risk, to go ahead and try to change?

The old adage goes, "Sometimes things have to get worse before they get better." That's one of the most painful parts of wanting to help a friend or a client. It is so frustrating to watch someone avoid changes that would make life more enjoyable and fulfilling. Since you have come to know the people I've used as examples, let me describe how I met some of them and how they also met their ostriches—face to face.

Cold Enough? Ken and Julie. I never saw Ken and Julie. I heard about them and their landlord/boiler problem from a friend. The concluding act of their ostrich drama came one day when the temperature dipped several degrees below zero and the boiler still wasn't working. Julie suddenly realized that nothing was being done about it— not by Ken, not by herself. She caught herself holding back going to the landlord because she had spent so much time discussing it with Ken as *his* responsibility. As it got colder, and as she felt a cold coming on, Julie realized that Ken wasn't about to complain to their landlord about the lack of heat. She was also at the point of really wanting to be warmer. Instead of another shared ostrich round of "When are *you* going to see him?" Julie got up the nerve to go see him herself. Yes, their apartment got warmer within several days, and, perhaps more important, Julie felt great about taking the task on herself and being successful at it. She told my friend one evening how delighted she was to find out she could be firm in a confrontation and have it turn out successfully. Of course, she and Ken did have an argument about her finally taking on the responsibility herself. Ken wanted the apartment warm, but he also wanted to be the forceful one who could take care of it.

These two are both in that middle ground of locus of control, and unsure of whether they want things done for them or not. Ken did not like the implication of Julie's behavior that said, "You couldn't handle it, so I did." But everything he had *not* done told her that that was the case.

Their situation is fairly straightforward. Ken and Julie had spent months building a sandpile of avoidance and deception that, unknown to both of them, ended up as ostrich territory. The only tool that was available to urge the ostrich from the sand was the temperature, an outside impetus that could no longer be ignored. It got cold; Julie got sick. Being cold finally caused Julie more pain than did her fears of confronting the landlord and testing her ability to be assertive. The lesson in the story of Julie and Ken is that the earlier you deal with your Ostrich Complex the better. The best time to start is now, before the pain gets any greater.

Fighter for Truth, Justice, and...: Walter. Unlike Deirdre, Walter came to see me involuntarily. His problems at work and at home had reached the point of disruption. They were attracting more attention than he could handle. His work colleagues began mentioning his run-down appearance, even to nicknaming him their "favorite zombie." Several people each day would ask him if things were all right, if there was something he would like to talk over with them. Of course there was—Jessica. Walter's anxiety had become so overwhelming, however, that he would only stare back at them with a glazed look, confirming their suspicions that, indeed, something was severely wrong. Walter's ostrich was so clever it had him convinced that when others offered to help, they were really trying to ease him out of the office under the guise of friendliness.

One day he reluctantly acceded to his wife's demands that he see their family doctor. That doctor listened to the symptoms and sent Walter to me. Well, you know ostriches. That one did not like the idea of having to confront the problem it was protecting. Walter made one appointment and then called the day before and cancelled. The relief from the cancellation didn't last long, however, and he called several days later to reschedule. When he did come in, it was evident that Walter had not slept well for quite some time.

Walter's situation needed a treatment as intense as the pain he was feeling. We scheduled three daily appointments to get a good start in our analysis of what was going on in his life. A few days later, he was grappling with the idea of going in to talk with his supervisors. We had been through some of the same questions, charts, and tests that you have in this book, and Walter had decided that the ambiguous situation at work was the root problem he needed to solve.

Just knowing what the problem was did not make his fears dissolve, but it was a necessary first step. Our task was to get Walter to the point of actually being able to go in and face the possibility that his worst fears would be realized, that Jessica really was being trained to replace him. That process took several weekly sessions. I learned the results when a messenger came to my door one Saturday morning with a bottle of champagne and a simple note that said, "Whew! I did it! Thanks. Walter."

I called him up and was delighted to find out from his wife (Walter was still sleeping) that Walter had gone in to see his vice-president the day before. He ignored the sick feelings we had anticipated would be there; he avoided the procrastination traps we had diagrammed; and he overcame the possibility of getting angry and making his boss defensive by using the dialogue we had practiced. His boss had been quite pleased that he came in because he, himself, had been meaning to set up an appointment with Walter to find out what was troubling him. Jessica had shared her worries about Walter's health with their mutual boss. He was concerned that Walter couldn't handle the stress of being the new section head—while Jessica took a similar position at one of their branches in another city.

Somewhere an ostrich sat with more sun shining in its eyes than it really wanted.

For Walter, making a first appointment to see me was an expression of his Ostrich Complex. His second call was not. He found that even though his ostrich had altered his perception of everything, from who controlled his life to how valuable he was as a person, he could still turn the tables. Walter was an achiever, a person who wanted to be responsible for what happened to himself, someone who reacted against perceived injustice. This time the injustice was being done to him by himself. His reaction, though delayed, was similar to his reaction anytime he faced unfairness: He fought it.

An Enthusiastic Ally: Ted. I met Ted while giving a presentation on the costs of the ostrich at work to a group of mid-level corporate managers. I had been invited to address the group by the president of a small electronics manufacturing company that had just gone public. Since the time that he and I had worked together on de-ostriching his company, he had been one of my most vocal cheerleaders. He would tell groups that finding the ostriches in his previously inefficient and debt-ridden company had gained him more than all of his production changes combined.

I told them my tennis racquet story as part of my presentation. I told them about how I ostriched my need to get a new one, worrying, instead, about fixing something that couldn't be fixed. During the question and discussion phase, Ted stood up and told a similar story about his own ostrich behavior. He told us that he was close to retirement and that he couldn't bring himself to draw up a will, a problem businessmen frequently ostrich. Ted laid out a complete and accurate description of his own ostriched problem, using my racquet story as his framework. Few people, I've found, grasp the ostrich concept as quickly as Ted did in that lecture. He told the group that he had been searching for a way to avoid looking at retirement just as I had been ostriching my need for a new racquet. He asked me what I recommended, so we used his situation as a model for talking about similar problems that people from other companies might have and disussing how they and their employees could become ostrich-free.

When I ran into Ted several months later, he confided that he had two goals in telling his story to his colleagues. One was that it just felt good to get it off his chest. The second was a subtle attempt to show his business associates that recognizing an ostriched problem and taking steps—including the difficult one of asking for help—isn't a confession of personal weakness. Revealing the truth in front of his colleagues, Ted had showed them and himself how strong he really was.

We became instant allies and friends. He began collecting stories of the ostrich costs in various companies and made the information available to me as part of my ongoing research and analysis. He helped me develop a data base for the Ostrich Complex that is the best proof I can think of for using ostrich-freeing methods as management-improvement techniques or planning techniques. They're much the same as relying on a calculator rather than doing all the math in your head. Ted, like the president of the electronics firm and numerous others, proved to me that my techniques could be developed on a much larger scale. The proof came as firms began to chart definite increases in productivity, as well as a decrease in absenteeism and illness—the two clearest signs of stress resulting from unchallenging, undefined, or unfulfilling work.

From Inequitable to Indispensable: Margaret. I met Margaret under similar circumstances. I had gone to address a small group at Margaret's company. Unlike Ted,

Margaret didn't stand up and make a public statement about her Ostrich Complex, nor did she come to see me professionally. Remember she scored in the internal locus of control and somewhat passive directions on the Personality Profile. In keeping with her own style, Margaret, instead, went to the library and her local book store to read some of the research and books I had mentioned during my talk. Then she went on to draw up a plan of action to deal with both sides of the ostriched problem as she now saw it, the external inequity in salary and her internal anxieties about confronting the facts.

Margaret did find a way to confront her boss. She chose, as we had role-played, a moment when it was clear to everyone how essential she had become to the company. She immediately got her equal pay for her equal work. In addition, Margaret found that colleagues around the office, even people she scarcely knew, were showing her more respect as she walked by or stood next to them in the elevator. The men began to take her more seriously, and the women began asking her for advice on their personal as well as career difficulties. A hard-headed and achievement-oriented person, Margaret attained what she sought once she saw that her problem had a name and a habitat. She could no longer make excuses, so she took swift action.

I found out about all this months later when I came back to Margaret's company for a follow-up visit. "Just like the insect man rechecks my house after his treatment," she joked. Margaret came up to me in the lobby and shared her story with me. It was one of those wonderfully gratifying experiences that are so rare.

Margaret came up with an excellent answer to the question: How bad do things have to get before you finally break out of your paralysis and do something? Her answer: If there's paralysis to break out of, things are already bad enough. And she reminded me of words I had used that struck home to her: If you don't value yourself enough to ask others for what you feel is fair, why should they have much regard for you?

The Downtrodden: Glenn. Glenn did end up in my office, but like so many ostriching people, not specifically at first to take care of his ostrich. Glenn didn't know he had one. He came in for vocational counseling. He was thinking seriously of changing jobs, possibly even returning to school and switching careers. He came to see me because he couldn't quite put his finger on what that other career might be. He was so eager to rid himself of Mr. Stevens that he would have jumped at anything I suggested.

Glenn described his frequent run-ins with his boss and his growing disillusionment with what had first seemed like such a promising team. As Glenn listed his grievances, I could see how much collecting he'd been doing. His tales of woe slowed as he started to hear what he was telling me about his career.

"You know," he said, "I'm beginning to think there's more to this than just old Stevens. Do you think there might be something I'm missing out on, some move I'm not making?"

Glenn's ostrich must have shuddered to hear part of its comfortable hole beginning to cave in. Glenn was starting to see that he was at least partially to blame in the difficulties he was having with Stevens because he was refusing to face their cause. The focus of our conversation changed from a search for a new career to a search for ways of handling his current career and turning his present job into what he had hoped it would be.

The Hopeless Romantic: Roy. I met Roy in a very different way; it was one of those awkward situations at a cocktail party that psychologists, like physicians or lawyers, often run into. Someone starts talking theory and ends up asking, "Well, what should *I* do, Doc?"

Roy had overheard a conversation that some of the other guests and I were having about relationships and came floating over. As he spoke, I could tell from his words and from the alcohol fumes that surrounded him that he was hurting.

"You a shrink?" he asked. "Gimme yer office number—I wanna talk to you." I handed him a card; he stuffed it into his shirt pocket and moved away. I doubted he would even know the next morning why he had that card.

A few days later, Roy called and came in. He started talking before he sat down—about Shirley. He had come to complain about her. He wanted to tell me how angry he was at her and to ask my advice on how to straighten *her* out. He had picked me as someone new on whom he could dump his story about how badly he was treated, and who could explain to him what *her* problem was. He was hoping I could give him something he could use against Shirley, probably as soon as he left my office. Roy found, as you probably have by now, that I don't play that way.

I asked Roy one question when he had finished his story. "She seems to give you a lot of pain. But some glue keeps you tied to her. Why can't you forget about her?"

He slid forward in his seat. For a moment, I couldn't tell if he meant to punch me, slam my desk, or just walk out.

Then he moved back in his chair, looked at his clenched hands and shook his head. "I don't know. I really don't. Maybe you can help me figure it out. I sure as hell can't make it out myself."

Both Roy and his ostrich had been roused by what I had said. His meek response was the first step toward evicting the ostrich from its comfortable home in Roy's relationships. He was soon on his way to realizing that all of his problems were not Shirley's doing and that his ostriched fears formed the glue that kept him stuck in such an unfulfilling relationship. He was soon on his way to recovering control over his own life.

THE FEAR OF CHANGE

We've seen in each of these situations that the fear of change is the number one obstacle to freeing the ostrich. We've also seen that it often takes a lot of pain before we're willing to take the chance and risk changing our lives.

People stay in jobs that they find degrading; they stay in relationships that are unrewarding, even painful. Why? Because we know all about life with our ostrich, yet we know nothing about what life would be like without it. We find comfort even in our discomfort. We don't know the answer to this question: Is there life after ostrich?

Yes, There Is. The risks that loom so large, at least from your personal view, are some of the *imaginary* problems that we discussed earlier. The risks and dangers you perceive in *the possibility of change* are like camouflage for the ostrich. But unlike military camouflage that needs you to change and repaint it with the seasons, the ostrich can produce an endless variety of shades and colors all on its own and without your being aware of it. That's because its raw material is your imagination.

Once you become inclined to take that risky step toward facing your problem, there is always the question of *when?* When should I start to do something about it? How about tomorrow? Is next week better yet? Maybe not as good as a month from now after things have settled down?

I usually find that the deeper in rationalization the problem is buried the further away in time you can schedule yourself to deal with it. Six months from now, or even a year, can easily seem like the best time to think about that bad relationship or miserable job. With the time problem disposed of so expeditiously, you can spin quite elaborate, sometimes even satisfying, daydreams about how you'll carry out that change. This accomplishes the ostrich's goal: Keeping you from asking one simple time question: Why not do it now?

Does that question send chills through your body? Does your stomach flip-flop when you just read the question? Those symptoms are normal so don't worry—about that.

The ostrich doesn't like words like *now,* so my next suggestion will make it uncomfortable. My suggestion is that the present, meaning right now, today, this hour, this minute—*right where you are standing or sitting at this moment*—is the time to do something. That something may be merely to identify the problem and recognize that the pain can only get worse. Or that something may be strong action. Delay is the ostrich's first survival tactic as well as its last line of defense. In truth, though, what will you be telling yourself about this same problem in six months or a year? Will you be saying, "I wish I'd done something back then?" If that's true, do it now and give yourself the additional better life that you deserve.

You don't have to be struck by a bolt of lightning before making a change. *You* can bring *yourself* to make that choice. After all, that's whose life we're talking about anyway: yours. In fact, if you've read this far in this book, you've been bringing yourself along for quite a while. I've only been tracing the road map for you; you've been doing the work. Now you are at the point of decision. Are you going to get rid of that ostrich *now?* Or at least *start* freeing yourself from it?

If you answered yes to either of those questions you're ready to move ahead. Earlier I asked you four questions about fear and dealing with your ostrich. Let me ask you four more questions now. A friend of mine calls these my "screwing up your courage" formula. Take a sheet of paper, answer these questions in writing, and tuck the paper into this book at the end of this chapter.

1. What do you fear the future would be if your own ostrich were set free?

2. What are the *good and bad* results that would occur if you did change your ostrich behavior?

3. What do you think you will *gain* if you change? At work? In interpersonal relationships? In your community or home? And what do you stand to *lose?*

4. What is the *net result* of setting your ostrich free?

I will bet you the price of this book that if you've answered these four questions honestly, the net result comes out in favor of doing something rather than staying with your ostrich. That's how confident I am that your ostrich is a parasite you really don't want to keep around— once you realize how it's messing up your life.

The normal fear of change. I'm closing this chapter by telling you how normal the fear of change is. It's not caused solely by the Ostrich Complex. It's a natural, common, and often useful part of our human psyche. Most of the time a healthy fear of change helps keep individuals and organizations running smoothly. After all, there are thousands of behavior patterns, social conventions, physical habits, and practices at home and at work that have been adopted by people because they work. "Tried and true" is often an extremely useful adage.

The Ostrich Complex, however, takes a normal reaction, perfectly reasonable in the right circumstances, and applies it in the wrong circumstances. When you can see that ostriching is an *inappropriate* response, you are ready to see that it has to be changed. You can move ahead: one, two, three.

- Recognize that the Ostrich Complex paralyzes effective decision-making;
- Decide to do something about it;
- Do it now.

Many techniques that can help are discussed in the next

chapter, but without the process I just mentioned they all add up to zero. The basic tools remain your realization and decision. With them you have an excellent chance of digging out.

Chapter 9

Techniques for Becoming Ostrich-Free

You've decided to change. Great! You've decided to face your ostrich squarely and yank its head from the sand. "That's all very well," you may be thinking, "but how do I do it? How do I shake loose from something that's been a part of me for so long?" Part of the ostrich's grip on you is a result of such thoughts, and worry that you are incapable of doing anything about it. You can. And you will with the help of the techniques that I've gathered together into this chapter for you.

As we discussed several pages ago, one of the most frightening things about change—particularly change that just might bring about improvements—is that you may think some dramatic makeover process is necessary. You may feel it is just too much to undertake and want to give up and continue with your old ways.

But we can divide the process of *change* into smaller parts using the same approach we've applied to the Ostrich Complex itself. In this chapter, I'm going to describe many specific change techniques that are appropriate for coping with the most stubborn Ostrich Complex. But remember that it's just as important to know *when* to use a given technique as it is to know *what* technique to use. So first we'll look at some general rules for freeing yourself from the ostrich.

GENERAL OSTRICH CHANGE STEPS

The following four steps are basic to most of the behavioral change views in psychology.[12] As you go through the specific change techniques, use these steps as an overview to each one. No matter which specific technique you choose for your own personal ostrich, the steps in using it are these:

Step 1. Define the Problem. Just what is wrong, anyway?

Step 2. Examine the Solutions You Have Tried in the Past. List them and see what, if anything, they have in common, and what their results have in common. Ask yourself if the solutions you typically apply are really a part of the problem. Do they add to its severity? Were these "solutions" really kinds of ostriching?

Step 3. Define Concrete Changes you would like to bring about. Be specific; don't hedge here. If you can't tell yourself exactly how you want things to be different, it will be difficult for you to pick the best ways to work on the problem.

Step 4. Set Out a Clear Plan of Action to achieve this change. Give your plan specific stages and attainable goals—and a specific schedule.

SPECIFIC OSTRICH CHANGE TECHNIQUES

I have my favorites among the ones that follow; my clients and friends have theirs. Our lists do not always overlap. That means that the techniques are here for your selection. You may want to try one or more now, and try another one later when it feels appropriate. They are all good. So, here are specific change techniques for your consideration—and use.

ACTION LIST: DECIDING WHAT TO DO FIRST

Make a *short* to-do list for a *limited* period of time, usually not more than one day. List the tasks in the order that they need to be done and check each off as it is completed. The *action list* is extremely useful when you are in high-pressure situations, at conferences, or involved in a job requiring a complex number of irregular individual trips, communications, delegations, or combination of these. The list is great for planning special events, expeditions, or for handling emergencies that can be cleared up in a series of progressive steps.

When you use this method, you must stick to the basic rule that nothing else be done until everything on the list has been dealt with in some way (see *time management* and other list-cleaning techniques). If you do approach the action list in this strict manner, then *triage* (a quick sorting of new incoming items into those that *do* need to be dealt with as emergencies) may help you with the process. But watch to be sure that your emergencies don't make your action list just another to-do list. The most important word here is *action*.

The action list was one of the ways Deirdre organized her anti-ostrich campaign. Instead of seeing everything she had to do as equally urgent, she was able to sort out those parts of the cases that *had* to be done first. In addition, Deirdre was able to analyze her tasks and delegate aspects of the cases that didn't really need her personal attention.

ADVERTISING: MAKING YOUR NEEDS KNOWN

Don't conceal your concerns—*advertise*. More than one salesman I know turns an obvious physical defect into a distinguishing characteristic by drawing attention to it when most people would try to conceal it. That is why you so often see salesmen using as a sales technique ridiculous props, outlandish clothing, or exaggerating a physical blemish or handicap they may have.

Walter used this technique to help himself out of his bind. When he went in to confront his superiors about Jessica, he didn't just want to know what they had to say about her. We had *role-played* the possibilities so he felt comfortable opening up just enough to them. He decided to tell them straight away that he was anxious about having to ask his questions. He didn't go into great detail, but he did let them know enough of what troubled him so they would understand, and he did it in such a calm manner that they could not look upon it as a sign of weakness or ineptitude. Walter's advertising campaign helped him yank his ostrich's head from the sand. Like a big corporation, he turned his concern into a well-thought-out message and made it known to the people who could respond to it.

ANGER: USING ITS ENERGY

Anger is one of the most difficult emotions to master. It can become a terrible adversary, a squandered opportunity, or a powerful tool. Some companies adopt the philosophy that "nothing unifies employees like a common enemy" and deliberately set out to anger employees with the goal of producing employee togetherness. Though this philosophy may work in theory, putting it into corporate practice rarely works because it is too difficult to control, too hard to direct, and too frequently misplaced.

In old Japan, people believed that anyone who died full of unsatisfied rage could put a dangerous and powerful curse on the object of his hatred, a belief that came in handy in keeping the amount of outrageous behavior to a minimum. The story told is about a warrior about to be executed who announces his intention to hex his chief enemy, who is present at the execution. The enemy laughs in his face, refusing to believe that his victim has the strength of will to cast an effective curse. The laughter, of course, makes the victim even more angry. The enemy finally admits that he will believe the curse if the victim agrees to give him a sign by biting a nearby rope at the moment he is beheaded.

The sword falls. The head leaps from the victim's shoulders and bounces to the rope, which it bites furiously. Upon seeing this, the enemy laughs again, for all of the victim's final hatred has gone into proving the power of his will. No anger is left for the curse.

Although things are not so dramatic in our world, the principle is still valid. Some call it venting or discharging anger, as though anger were pent-up pressure or an electric charge. In essence, it is. We feel the pressure build up, often to the point where we displace our anger onto "the last straw," someone who really doesn't deserve the curse we put on him or her. But we've not released anger onto the appropriate target, or onto something that can take the pressure and not be hurt.

Some people punch pillows; others cry; still others release anger through sports. These techniques work to varying degrees for each of us. The principles in releasing anger, however, are these: First, get a clear idea of your target. Pinpoint the real reason for your anger. Is it your own inability to do something as well as you would like? Is it what someone else is doing that you feel is unfair? The second step is then to release that anger in the best way for you. That means if just releasing it is most important, throw pillows, let the tears flow, or slam tennis balls around. If changing the situation that led up to it is more important, however, you must develop a strategy to use the energy in your anger to produce that change.

ASSERTIVENESS: GETTING WHAT YOU WANT

Being assertive is not the same as being aggressive, which is often a form of angry behavior, typically motivated by a desire to seem powerful. *Assertiveness* is motivated, rather, by a desire for effective action and a decision to define exactly what you want and what you do not want from someone else. It involves a clear plan for attaining the goal you desire and understanding how others will act in the process. Being assertive means that you can identify what the problem is and then work out in your own mind *how you can present it* without hurting another person. Think about assertiveness as a three-step process as you plan your approach in dealing with someone else. Your first step is to tell the other person, "This is how I feel." Then you say, "This is what has happened." Your third step is to ask, "What can we do about it?" Being assertive and being sensitive go hand in hand. Before you move from one step to the next, you assess how the other person has reacted to the previous one. You may need to explain your feelings at length, for example, before the other person is ready to hear what has happened.

BEHAVIOR MODIFICATION: CHANGING YOUR WAYS

Behavior modification is not a single technique but rather a program for employing several techniques in tandem. The process involves the following steps:

- **Define** the behavior you want to change, what you want to change it to, and what your available techniques are for making that change.
- **Use Successive Approximations.** Break the behavior you want to change into small, easily managed parts. Treat it as you would any new skill, as when you first learned to ride a bike. Put training wheels on your new behavior at the beginning and then take them off as you get better at it.
- **Decide** precisely what rewards and punishments you plan to use in order to rid yourself of the undesired behavior and develop a more desirable one.
- **Determine** the contingencies: What are the precise conditions under which you'll reward or punish yourself?
- **Monitor** your progress. Chart your results so that you can determine periodically how your program is going.
- **Learn** from failures. Treat each failure as a learning experience. Evaluate what went wrong and modify your program as needed.

I once worked with Mike, a writer who almost always missed his deadlines for delivering material to his publisher. We designed a behavior-modification program specifically to get him to meet a time schedule. Mike agreed to make five $100 checks out to various charities. He then agreed to five weekly deadlines each for a portion of his work; one check would be mailed to a charity for each of the deadlines he missed. It didn't work. I mailed three of the checks before we spent some time trying to understand what was going wrong. It seemed that Mike was able to rationalize sending the money—and missing our deadlines—

by telling himself, "Well, I really should be contributing more than I do to charity, anyway." Once we understood this, Mike wrote new checks, this time made out to organizations he disliked the most, the ones he found *least* worthy of his charity. After that change in his program, Mike never missed one of our deadlines.

So don't expect to be right on target right away. Like Mike, you may not as of yet have found the most effective reward or punishment. Or you may give up too soon because you alternate between expecting too much and too little. The perfectionistic ostrich tries to sabotage things in this way just to get you to stop. If you persist, however, you'll find that you gradually are making the changes you want. As you keep up with your own program, you'll find that it's becoming more and more finely tuned, until finally it becomes what you hoped to accomplish.

BREAKING THE LOOP: DARING TO DO

We are often paralyzed by the unthinkable. Sometimes that unthinkable is terrifying; but often it's not much more than just, well, unthinkable. For example, it's a gray, rainy day, damp, chilly, and dark. What is there to do but hibernate? Many just talk about how miserable it is, to others and to themselves. Of course, such talk doesn't make it any better for anyone. What about *breaking that loop*? What about looking at what there is that could be accomplished on a day such as this one? You can look upon it as a chance to relax or as a welcome end to a drought. Try expressing some of the possible positive thoughts to others. At first, they may give you a sideways glance, but I'll bet that they will come around to saying, "Yes, maybe it isn't so bad, after all."

Two people can look at the exact same event and interpret it differently.[13] They also then react to it differently, emotionally and physiologically. The "It's miserable" person will probably feel depressed, while the "Great for the plants" person will feel enthusiasm for life.

Certainly not all problems can be reinterpreted in a positive light. But *most* of them have upbeat aspects if you look at them.

Attitudes are quite powerful in shaping our emotions and the emotions of the people with whom we work and live. Julie used breaking the loop to get their heater repaired. One really cold day became a stimulus to action and she found she was able to do something positive.

DISTANCING: AS THOUGH IT'S HAPPENING TO SOMEONE ELSE

An excellent technique for couples involved with a shared ostrich is *distancing,* though it can also be modified for business situations. In using this technique the couple, whether lovers or boss and employee, step back from their problem and talk about *it* as though they were outside observers. They discuss what *that couple* is doing; what *he* and *she* want from the other; what each fears from the *it*; and what *they* can do to break free of their ostrich. This allows the couple to discuss the problem in a non-threatening way and can later lead to a free exchange of *"I"* statements. Distancing is one of my favorite techniques. Sometimes telling someone else what I don't like, and vice versa, just doesn't work for me. Distancing allows us to discuss the same issues without feeling threatened. We can then move our discussion into the personal since the topic and the issues have become clearer.

DISTASTEFUL TASKS: DOING THE WORST FIRST

If a job is a *distasteful task* but is something that needs to be done now, do it first. If it can be done later and you decide to delay it, schedule it first for a later specific time when you know you will get to it. Do the worst first. The anxiety of having it hanging over your head like the sword of Damocles will be dissolved, and you can undertake other tasks with a more relaxed attitude.

Marie, our friend who could not get her own taxes done, used this approach. It meant doing her own taxes *before* spending time on the little easy tasks that kept her too busy. Marie procrastinated when it came to completing her own taxes by tackling everything from sweeping out the garage to taking her newspapers to a recycling center. Scheduling—and completing—her income tax preparation first was difficult, but that's what we'd worked on during our sessions, how rough it would be and the pains and gains from doing it. It saved her months of anxiety and a good sum in tax penalities. Ted used this technique, as well, to get his will written. Remember, if your ostrich has that distasteful task seeming too large to manage, use other techniques such as *divide and conquer* to get yourself started.

DIVIDE AND CONQUER:
BREAKING IT INTO PIECES

When you set out your goals, the most important ones may seem so impossible to accomplish that you bypass them. The easier goals are seductive just by their simplicity. More important aims never get met because they never get planned. You ostrich them, bury them until another day when you feel more ambitious. You can deal with this problem this way: Take your most important goal and examine it carefully. Then *divide* it into manageable segments that you can realistically *conquer*. Make each of these segments a new goal in and of itself. Figure out what the first one is, and then break that down until you come up with a step that you can actually finish *today*. But also make sure that you know what steps you have to take tomorrow. And don't allow yourself to ostrich the next step when tomorrow comes. Rationalizing like this: "You really did a lot yesterday moving toward your most important goal. Why not wait awhile and see what happens from what you did yesterday?" can be a tempting notion, so beware.

You may think that your most ambitious goal is too complex even to start on. Think about the seemingly impossible goals that have been realized by breaking the tasks down into hundreds or even thousands of doable steps. Consider the manned space program—thousands of people worked at that for over twenty years. Or some of the classic battles in history. Or building a house from scratch, as we discussed in an earlier chapter. Each goal had to be divided so that the difficulty of the task could be overcome.

Nancy and Nick used this technique when it came to tackling the problems they'd been putting off facing. Examining their entire relationship felt overwhelming. Strange for both Nancy and Nick, however, was that they had each mastered the divide and conquer technique as a business skill. Their ostriched fears, however, kept them from applying it to their personal lives. Instead of needing to learn how to use this technique, Nancy and Nick had to learn to be objective enough about their marriage to use the technique once again.

DOING IT: WHOSE JOB IS IT ANYWAY?

Do those things that need to be done *by you*. If you need to change the oil in your own car and there's no mechanic within 1,000 miles, go ahead and do it. But if you're doing it without thinking what it will cost you in time and energy—and what else you're avoiding doing—then rethink doing it. The money you save by doing too much yourself may cost you more in the long run. I've worked with too many middle-level managers who felt that they were making themselves valuable to the company by doing everything themselves. They found out the hard way that they were wrong. Spending time on the little tasks impressed no one. Their superiors noticed only that they then did not have the time or energy for the important tasks. If you do have things that must be done, and you are absolutely certain that you are the one who *must* do it, don't delegate, delay, or dump. Go ahead—do it.

DOUBLE-DUTY LETTERS: PUTTING IT INTO WORDS AND FOCUS

After seeing Roy a few times, I had him write one of these to Shirley. I told him to pour it all out in the letter, to tell her everything he thought and felt about her, the good and the bad. He wrote a masterpiece, summing up everything in a way he hadn't been able to do in our sessions. He recalled how promising their early time together had been. And he told her how bitter and fed-up he'd become. He was still angry when he brought the letter to my office. Then I told him *not* to send it. It had already done its *double duty*. It helped Roy *express* the feelings that he had kept inside, and it had also given him a way to bring those feelings into *focus*. Double-duty letters are excellent ways for anyone to express feelings and help bring them into focus: Employees can clarify in their own minds what they want from the boss; managers can become clearer about what they feel is wrong with their own positions and their relationships with their employees; children can feel free to examine feelings they have about Mom, Dad, and school; and those in relationships, like Roy, can safely express their buried feelings.

EASY TASKS: THEY STILL NEED DOING

Don't let *easy tasks* fool you. This is a misnomer invented by the ostrich. There is no such thing as an easy task; there are only tasks that don't cause you as much anxiety or fear as others. Once something becomes a task for you, it has all the potential dangers of the ones that you dread. It's best to treat one that seems too easy as a *distasteful task* just in case you've been deceived.

"ENOUGH" DECISIONS: PERFECTION IS TOO MUCH TO ASK

Do you wait until you've gathered 100 percent of the information that you need before attacking a problem or completing a task? How can you ever expect to get it all? How can you know everything about a problem? You can't. It's that simple. Your ostrich may push you in that direction, but such perfectionism only leads to more procrastination. Deirdre followed my recommendation that she complete her first legal case when she had 85 percent of the information she needed. She found that it was *more than enough* to enable her to do an outstanding job. You'll find that to be the case, too. Be realistic in facing your projects—don't allow yourself to spend so much time in preparation there's no time left to do the job.

GUIDED IMAGERY: SEEING AHEAD

We seldom appreciate the power of our minds to make images that influence our actions. Advertisers do—and it works. Therapists use it frequently for treating extreme phobias—and it works. It took Walter only a few sessions with me to be able to imagine himself leaving his house in the morning and then to imagine himself being relaxed while at the office. *Guided imagery* and *role-playing* are both powerful tools that allow you to practice a new behavior without actually having to be in the threatening situation.

The key in guided imagery is to relax and imagine yourself in the stressful situation, using the behavior you want to use to deal effectively with it. Think about the problem as a series of increasingly anxious events, such as Walter's: getting dressed and thinking about work; leaving home; arriving at the office; being in his own office; going into his boss's office; starting the discussion with his boss; and so on. If you tense up, take a break and then relax again. Then repeat imagining an event lower in your anxiety hierarchy. Imagine that event as you relax and then move up your listing to events that make you increasingly more anxious. In this way, you're learning to associate relaxation with each of those events rather than the anxiety that has become a habit.

HALF LISTENING: ALL OR NOTHING AT ALL

Don't. If it's not worth all your attention, it's not worth any.

HUMOR: WHEN IT'S ALL RIGHT TO LAUGH

Humor can be a help or a hindrance in dealing with an Ostrich Complex. John Dryden, the Restoration writer, said, "Men (and women) aim rightest when they shoot in jest." Beware of the overuse of humor directed at others in trying to handle your problems. Too often you will be caught up in releasing stored anger, and what you try to express humorously will come across as not too veiled hostility. Such sarcastic anger leads to blocked communication, not to effective problem-solving.

By all means, however, do keep your humor about you when examining and dealing with your ostrich. Develop a true sense of being able to laugh at what you do in addition to laughing at what others do in living with an ostrich. Some of the machinations we use to protect our feathered friend are genuinely funny. So relax and laugh; let what you usually treat too seriously be a humorous part of your new ostrich-free personality.

"I" STATEMENTS: FIRST PERSON POSITIVES

Most therapy approaches want the client to be able to make what are called in psychological jargon "*I statements.*" These are clear messages about "how I feel," made without blaming the other person for what has happened. Such personal statements are very effective ways of expressing the emotions that are often buried alongside the ostrich. Glenn found Mr. Stevens much more receptive to his concerns when he presented them as "I feel . . ." rather than attacks phrased as "You made me . . ." The ostrich behaviors of collecting or denying the problem often come with statements such as, "You jerk! Look how you made me feel!" "I" statements allow you honestly and assertively to say, "I am feeling this way. Let's look at what happened and what we can do about it."

INTERRUPTIONS: AVOID THEM

If you have a door, close it. If you have an answering machine, use it. If you don't have a door to close, try a sign that tells potential interrupters that you are not available. If someone does get through, either in person or on the phone, give him or her a *definite* time when you will be available. Or better yet, let him share the responsibility. Give him a time when he can call or come back. It means one less bit of clutter on your desk.

LISTS: SETTING PRIORITIES

If you are a list person, start by making one list of everything that you feel you have to do. Do it just to give yourself an overview of your situation; but *don't*, at this point, try to do what's on your list. Now go back over all of those items and assign each one a value. Think about the needed investment for each one in terms of time, effort, and money versus what you see as the potential— and probable—yield. What will you get out of it compared to what you have to put in?

You'll probably find that only about 20 percent of the tasks hold about 80 percent of the value for you. These should obviously be given higher values than the others. Rate the tasks as follows: *A*: Must be done now: *B*: Important but does not need to be done right now; *C*: Can be delayed, delegated, or dumped. Some of my clients find it helpful to think of these values as three desk drawers: The *A* items go in the top drawer, the *B* into the middle, and the *C* into the bottom one. *Doing* always starts with the *A* drawer and stays there until they're completed. And always do the highest-return items first—even if they are the most difficult.

LOGICAL NEGOTIATION: GOOD FOR ME AND FOR YOU

It is logical to negotiate so that each person in the discussion gets what he or she wants—at least, as much as possible. The more balanced the result is in terms of what each gets from the negotiation, the more likely a mutually satisfactory relationship. As with the *self-agenda, logical negotiation* involves your making a conscious effort to list what the other person wants and needs from your relationship in addition to listing what you want and need. Figure out what's in it for the other person if he gives you much of what you're seeking. Then make him aware of what he stands to gain; he may not have thought of it. You can then both come out of the negotiation as winners.

MOVING AWAY: GETTING A NEW PERSPECTIVE

If a solution does not seem to be working, review what's been going on. If the solution is making things worse, cut back on how you are implementing it. Even consider trying its opposite.

When Roy realized that his solution to his problem with Shirley was not working, he took a different approach. The more he had tried to work it out, the worse things got. Changing to the opposite, which for Roy meant not pursuing Shirley and a solution, didn't make the relationship any more wonderful, but it didn't make it any worse, either. Roy felt that slowing his pursuit gave him time to examine what he wanted and did spread the discomfort around. One evening Shirley called to ask if they could get together to talk about "it." That was the first time Roy could remember that she had ever acknowledged that there was an "it," meaning their relationship and all of its concomitant problems. "I wasn't playing hard to get or anything," Roy told me later. "I just had a lot to do that started to seem more important. I guess I really have changed."

OSTRICH BOX: YOUR PROCRASTINATION FILE

An *ostrich box* is where you put all the things that you are most likely to ostrich—that telephone call message you hate to return; that bill that you always put off paying; the task that makes you nervous just to think about. Use a special file drawer, a colored file folder, or even a real box for these items. Use your ostrich box especially for incoming materials so that you can sort out the tasks you have negative responses to as soon as they appear. It's a good warning about where to expect trouble next. Executives who have an ostrich box on their desks not only model effective problem-solving for their employees, they also get more done themselves.

OSTRICH MEMO: PROFIT VS. PROCRASTINATION

The *ostrich memo* is a memo form that I've designed just for those "likely-to-ostrich" tasks. Copy the form and *attach it* to anything that you might ostrich, whether it's a file folder, a telephone call to return, or a major project. Check off the appropriate boxes on the form and then use the memo as your reminder. Decide if that task should be delegated, and if so to whom? Should it be postponed? Until when? Or should it just be dumped? Then arrange the tasks that you've tagged with an ostrich memo in priority order, most-distasteful-for-the-most-gain at the top.

PERSIAN RUG PLOY: THE REAL IMPORTANCE OF BEING PERFECT

This technique is a good one for overcoming perfectionism, an ostrich behavior with goals that are impossible to meet—and certainly not cost-effective. Make a deliberate mistake, a deliberate insignificant error, or let something go by that you would typically try to get perfect. Your mistake will still be under your control and yet will diffuse some of your ostriched anxiety. You will also see that a small mistake will usually go unnoticed or unremarked, thus demonstrating the pointlessness of worrying about doing everything perfectly. The *Persian rug ploy* derives from a custom among makers of Persian rugs. They traditionally make one deliberate error in each rug as an admission of inevitable human fallibility and to guard against the bad luck that follows arrogance.

PLANNED STRESS: TIME SLOT FOR TROUBLES

It sometimes helps to consolidate your high-stress tasks into a single block of time. In this way *you* decide to be

Techniques for Becoming Ostrich-Free

```
* * * * * * * * * * * * * * * * * * * * * * * * *
*                                               *
*           THE OSTRICH MEMORANDUM              *
*                                               *
*   DATE: _____                       *
*                                               *
*   TO:    Myself                                *
*                                               *
*   RE:    Identify or Attach Problem _____    *
*                                               *
*          _____        *
*                                               *
*                                               *
*   THIS IS: __ URGENT   __ HIGH      __ LOW      *
*                          PRIORITY     PRIORITY  *
*            (today)     (this week)  (next week) *
*                                               *
*          NOT WORTH AN OSTRICH MEMO _____     *
*                                               *
*   ACTION TO BE TAKEN:                          *
*                                               *
*   [  ] Delegate to: _____   *
*                                               *
*   [  ] Postpone until: _____   *
*                                               *
*   [  ] Phone to Set Meeting with: _____   *
*                                               *
*   [  ] Trash It in: _____ nearest waste basket *
*                                               *
*   [  ] Write/Dictate Response to: _____   *
*                                               *
*   [  ] Call Staff Meeting for: _____   *
*                                               *
*   [  ] Personally Confront: _____   *
*                                               *
*   [  ] Just Try to Ignore It: ____ good luck!  *
*                                               *
*   [  ] Other? _____   *
*                                               *
* * * * * * * * * * * * * * * * * * * * * * * * *
```

highly stressed at a certain time; stress doesn't get to sneak up on you and yell "Surprise!" *Planned stress* is the opposite of *scheduling recreation*.

RESISTANCE: SAYING NO SO YOU CAN GET TO YES

When things look and feel rough, and you've gotten tangled up in conflicting motives that leave you confused as to what to do next, *resist*. A bit of stubborn resistance to *everything* will help the unimportant tasks and issues separate themselves from the important ones. Resistance to whatever is pushing you around *now* acts like a filter and can help put you back in control of your life. Resistance means saying no to almost everything and then gradually letting the *A* tasks back into your schedule as your ideas of what is important become clear.

Resistance worked for Gary in overcoming some of the problems he had in expressing his anger. Gary, you remember, went from extremely shy to aggressive in trying to tell his boss what he wanted. His attempts didn't work and resulted in feelings of "What's the use?" To help sort out what he really wanted from a large number of confusing thoughts, Gary did nothing.

ROLE-PLAYING: PRACTICE IS THE BEST PREPARATION

Role-playing means practicing what to do in a threatening situation with the help of a friend or therapist who assumes the role of the person you will be confronting. With such practice, you can explore the options and be prepared to act flexibly so that you can stay in control regardless of what direction the encounter takes. Role-play the worst that is likely to happen, the best that could happen, as well as what you consider to be the most likely—the worst and the most likely rarely are the same even though they feel like it at times. No matter what the reality of the situation turns out to be, you will have faced the fears that could keep your ostrich hidden and have thought out in advance the very best maneuvers to cope with them.

Supervisors can use role-playing to decide on the most effective means to handle a difficult employee situation. Couples can use it so that each person becomes aware of the feelings that the other has about an ongoing problem. Many of the people you've met in this book found role-playing to be excellent preparation for the actual encounter.

A different way to use role-playing involves switching roles, a "You be me; I'll be you" variation. Therapists frequently use this type of role-playing with couples or with a child and parent. The basic idea behind switching roles is to "Walk a mile in the other person's moccasins." If you and the other person involved in the problem are present, you each change from playing yourself and play the role of the other as you discuss the problem. Each then tries to think, act, and feel as the other person does as you review the issues. Even if the other person who is involved in the problem isn't there with you for role-switching, you can have a friend play yourself while you assume the role of the other person in that specific encounter.

There's nothing like rehearsal, and the more realistic, the better.

SCHEDULES: YOUR TIME IS YOUR TIME

After getting your *A* tasks separated from the *B*'s and *C*'s, make a schedule. Organize one schedule for the month, another for the week, and yet another for the day. After completing that day, take a close look at your schedule. How much were you actually able to accomplish? Who put all those things on that schedule? Were they other people's demands? What can you learn from that review about how you make schedules and apply that to tomorrow's schedules? Review your weekly and monthly schedules in a similar way. You'll find that organization actually frees you to do the "fun" things you haven't had time for. And being more organized will help you feel *more* flexible rather than less so. Teach yourself to make a schedule that fits your needs so that you can live ostrich-free.

SCHEDULING RECREATION: R & R AS S.O.P.

"And on the seventh day He rested." When you make out your schedule, don't forget to reward yourself for your hard work by scheduling breaks and recreation. All too often we force ourselves into work schedules that we would never ask anyone else to attempt. Remember the law of diminishing returns. If you schedule only work, you will spend more time on a task than you will get in production and returns. You need "down time," some "R & R," just like everyone else. The last thing you can afford is the serious down time of sickness or burnout. And once you schedule those breaks, actually take them. Then return, on schedule, to your tasks.

SELF-AGENDA: POINTS TO MAKE

Every meeting has an agenda—the issues that those calling the meeting want to cover. But we each have our own agendas, as well, though all too often we keep ours hidden. When you go to a meeting, prepare an agenda in advance for yourself. This is as important in your personal life as it is in business. You need to know what you want to get out of a situation before you go into it.

When Roy did meet with Shirley about their relationship, he wasn't clear about what the details of her agenda were, though he'd gotten a general idea during their phone conversation. Roy and I drew up his agenda, however, made up of points that he wanted to cover, listed in the order of their priority. This is also how Margaret planned her confrontation with her boss. By making her own agenda, she formed a clear idea of what she wanted to cover in their meeting. Glenn also found this invaluable in his dealings with Mr. Stevens. I'll discuss—and show you—his self-agenda in Chapter Ten.

I'm not suggesting that you walk into meetings with sheets of agenda items, but do prepare one, even if you take in only a note card or two as your security blanket. We all have our own agendas, but when we let ourselves stray from them, the reasons are often ones determined by our ostrich.

SELF-REHEARSAL: TALKING TO YOURSELF

Self-rehearsal is the physical offshoot of *guided imagery*, and involves practicing your new desired behaviors by yourself—without a partner. Here you take on both roles instead of just one. It may sound a bit schizophrenic, but such "talking to yourself" is a safe way to get the feel of what might happen and how the other person may respond. Successful salespeople, such as Alan, who overcame a need to be perfect in his work, often use self-rehearsal before an important sales call. Alan uses the time driving to appointments to talk through the dialogue to come, playing both himself and his customer, as he rides in his car. Self-rehearsal helps him—and will help you—anticipate what is likely to happen and increase your control in any encounter.

STEW TIME: SIMMERING-DOWN PERIOD

I designed this one especially for Deirdre, who liked to sit in her office and stew about how hard everything was. It was too much to expect her to stop such behavior immediately, so I assigned her to a half hour of *stewing* each morning after which she had to tackle an *A* task. Within a week Deirdre had asked to cut her stew time to fifteen minutes. Within three weeks she was fully cooked and gave it up totally. She said, "I don't know how I *ever* put up with it!"

SUCCESS EXPERIENCES: REWARD YOURSELF

Arrange your schedule and your tasks so that you are always *successful* because you can always complete your scheduled tasks. If you schedule too much for yourself, you are letting your ostrich schedule failure for you instead.

TIME MANAGEMENT: YOUR TIME
REALLY IS YOURS

All ostriches share one characteristic: They are experts at messing up our ability to use time effectively and to our own satisfaction. Taking control of our time becomes very important in freeing ourselves from the Ostrich Complex. These next three techniques are "Three D's" that I picked up at an excellent workshop on *time management*. The most important of these is *delegate;* the other two are *dump* and *delay*.

Delegate. The ostrich hates to *delegate*. Yet what are the results of not delegating? They're obvious difficulties such as work overload, increased anxiety, and incomplete tasks, all very comfortable bedding for the ostrich. Think about Dwight D. Eisenhower when he was commanding the Normandy invasion in World War Two. Could he or any other general have handled that task without delegating thousands upon thousands of tasks to his subordinates? No. Did delegating make him any less of a leader? No. In fact, his ability to delegate emerged as his single most important skill. And the same has been true for business and political leaders throughout history.

Why then do people persist in stubbornly refusing to delegate when the pain from keeping all the work to themselves is so great? I have found that the main reasons lie in what we say to ourselves about giving work to another. Have you ever said one of these?

- I'll be less important if I have to give work to someone else (the fear of losing self-esteem).
- I'll have to admit that I can't get the job done (the fear of failure).
- Nobody else can do it as well as I can (perfectionism).
- I shouldn't be doing this anyway (collecting).
- I don't have the time now so I'll do it later (procrastination).
- It's not a very important job anyway (denial).

The underlying reason for these statements seems to be a fear of losing control over the situation. The truth is that delegating can actually give you more control over that situation. In fact, the more people you can delegate to, the more important your position is, because only powerful people can delegate.

Let me tell you about a less momentous event than World War Two that happened to me and my ostrich. Last year I left town without telling my answering service that I was unavailable. I told myself, "I'll only be gone for a day and a half so why should I delegate anything? I can handle it all easily." The service took my messages as usual. I wound up having to be gone an extra two days, however, before I remembered that no one knew I was unavailable. When I did call in, I found that one person had tried to reach me several times to get some information. According to my service, he was irate that I had not returned his calls.

My reaction was to become equally irritated. He had wanted a favor from me and had not even told me to call collect. That's a little thing, true, but I must admit that it did bother me. So I put off calling him until that time "when all calls are returned," and "all memos are answered," and all "I'll get to thats" are gotten to—*later*.

You can imagine the rest of the story. The longer I procrastinated returning his call, the more embarrassed I got about it and the harder it became to return his call. What saved me? Delegating. I had to call in to the executive secretary of the state psychological association for which I serve as executive director. Since the original call concerned the association, and since our secretary had access to a WATS line, I asked her to bail me out. She took the request as a compliment and ended up performing the task far more efficiently and faster than I would have. By the end of that day I had gotten to take a very heavy to-do out of the ones that I'd been collecting.

Delay. Doing things now is usually very important, but knowing what to put off is just as important. If the task doesn't need to be done now, and if doing it won't bring the highest possible return on your time and effort investment, then *delay* it to another specific time. Note that you haven't forgotten the job or denied that it needs to be done. What you've done here instead is to recognize its level of importance and then make a conscious decision to put it off until another time.

Dump. If you aren't going to do it, or delegate it, or delay it, then just *dump* it—now. Most of the tasks, memos, phone calls, social obligations, and et ceteras are things we didn't ask for to begin with. It's important to flag these items as soon as they first appear. Try to dispose of them immediately. Go ahead—make a decision. Open your mail while holding a wastebasket between your knees. Look at each item and think about what would happen if you tossed it right now. What's the worst thing that could happen—or would happen? I'll bet you can toss a lot more than you would have originally expected.

A friend of mine who is a documentary filmmaker has a very difficult time choosing among the thousands of feet of film that go into each of his final projects. Sometimes he has to take more than twenty hours of film and cut it into one that runs thirty minutes. Often 90 percent of his footage is excellent. His ostrich and he used to ponder for hours over each foot, worried that every piece of film would be the one that would make or break the project. He now has a sign over his editing bench that says "When in doubt, cut!" It's a formula that can benefit most of us. When you can't do it; and it doesn't seem like something you want to delegate; and it also doesn't seem like something you want to delay to a specific time, then dump it.

TRIAGE: TREAT THE NEEDIEST

Beware the emergency. Hospitals use *triage* to decide how to allocate scarce resources during times of crisis. It refers to a system designed to produce the greatest benefit from a limited amount of a commodity, such as medicine, food, or, for you, energy and attention. You must use your wits to decide how to allocate your own resources in dealing with ostriched problems. Many of the tasks that feel like emergencies will be *trivia*; others will be *C* problems that are presented as demands by someone else; some will be actual emergencies that need to take priority over already established *A* tasks. Consider each emergency in terms of energy versus gain and in light of what you know about your own ostrich.

TRIVIAL PURSUITS: FINDING THE TREES IN THE FOREST

Trivia is a type of ostrich confetti meant to distract you from what you know is important. The military calls this chaff. It consists of thousands of pieces of shiny and warm metal that planes and ships shower into the air when under missile attack. With the chaff in the air, the missile's guidance system gets confused and can't pick out the desired target. Your ostrich throws out trivia for the same reason. Its chaff is made up of little interruptions; of a feeling that "I ought to do just this little thing before I do my important work"; of friendly chats on the phone or anxiety about *C* value tasks that really can wait.

YOURS AND YOURS ALONE: CREATE YOUR OWN TECHNIQUE

A goal of any ostrich-change technique is to remove some of the paralysis that comes with the Ostrich Complex. I encourage all of my clients, whether they are dealing with individual concerns or with corporate issues, to let themselves think freely about ways to remove the ostrich from their midst. You may find a technique among those I've listed in this chapter that with just a little modification can work perfectly for you. Or you may be able to *create your own technique* and apply it to your specific situation. Both paths will reach the same end, that of setting you free from the Ostrich Complex.

A friend in publishing tells me of a manager who realized how much time he and the people in his organization were wasting in meetings. His technique? He removed the chairs from the meeting rooms so that people had to stand or lean while they talked. The result? Time spent in meetings was cut by more than half. Or you can take a research-produced fact and develop your own technique. For example, studies have shown that employees feel they gain more information about their company from discussions around the water cooler than directly from management.[14] One company used that fact to schedule "water cooler time" for its employees as part of their work schedule. Managers were then able to take a break along with their employees and share in the exchange of information around the water cooler. The ostrich is creative—so you must be, too.

ZEROING IN: TRY AND TRY AGAIN

Don't expect to get an exact focus on your target immediately. You'll probably undershoot or overshoot at first. Learn from your first attempts and try again. Misses are not failures; they are there to show the way.

We have looked at a long list of techniques for you to use in freeing yourself from your Ostrich Complex. You are now in the position of having to pick and choose from among them in order to design a behavior-change prescription just for you. That's what I call personalizing the Ostrich Prescription, and that's what we'll look at in the next chapter.

Chapter 10

Prescription Personalizing

This chapter is all about change techniques and you. It's about how you can decide which specific technique or set of techniques from Chapter Nine is best for overcoming your personal Ostrich Complex. You've taken the tests, filled out the forms, and answered many important questions about yourself. You have a pretty good idea of your own situation.

Not One for All and All for One. As you read in Chapter Six, I learned a tough lesson about prescribing generic solutions. Remember my early talks with Gary? That's when I prescribed the right therapeutic technique for the wrong person in the wrong situation. I learned from that experience that it is critical that *you* design your own behavior change program. Your ostrich is unlike all others and will probably not even stir when you try to remove it by using the wrong technique. I hope you also realized from reading about Gary's experiences that there is no predetermined answer that can be handed to you. The only right answer is *your* answer, the one you work out by yourself or in consultation with someone else.

The main problem is how to recognize the right answer, that is, the best technique when it (they) are in front of you. The key to solving this problem and avoiding more ostriching is to divide your big problem into the smaller ones that are its components. Find out what those small problems are and then go ahead and deal with them one at a time. By the time you're halfway through them, you'll be tackling two at a time and wondering why it took you so long when you started.

Your Tool Kit. Let's now discuss how to choose the change techniques that will help you get rid of your specific ostrich. Let's think about the behavior-change techniques in Chapter Nine as tools to help you dig out your ostrich. As with physical tools, some are better for certain situations than are others. You know that when you dig for an ostrich and you strike cement, you need to put your shovel away and use a jackhammer. And, conversely, when you're digging through loam, how much is a jackhammer going to help?

How do you identify the tool that you need for any given problem? You've already done much of the work in Chapter Seven by completing the summary pages. Now it's time to integrate those ideas. Remember, you can't change all ostrich problems at once. So for this step, look back at the ostrich problems you listed as the *ones you really want to change*. Think back—or look back—to what you wrote in Chapter Three and Chapter Four, just in case you feel you've misidentified the problem on which you want to work. Tackle only one ostrich problem at a time, so pick the one that you decide is "it."

Your Ostrich Goal Statement. A good way to pinpoint the ostrich you want to track down, dig up, and lose is by completing the Ostrich Goal Statement that follows. Since I asked you in Chapter Eight to analyze Deirdre's ostrich problem, I'm presenting her Goal Statement here for you to use in understanding how to complete yours. Hers is a good example of one that was filled out and then put into action.

DEIRDRE'S OSTRICH GOAL STATEMENT

Ostrich Problem. I am unable even to begin working on important legal cases.
It usually occurs when I sit down at my desk, or hear my colleagues talk about how smart I am, or even think about the cases.
I think I ostrich it because I'm afraid that I'm not as good when I'm in charge as when I follow orders; and what if I lose my first cases?
I would be confident of having successfully overcome this ostrich problem if I could just get started on my cases.

Now complete the one that follows for the problem you want to tackle. Describe as precisely as possible the context in which your ostrich problem occurs.

YOUR OSTRICH GOAL STATEMENT

Ostrich problem: _____

It usually occurs when I _____

_____

I think I ostrich it because I'm afraid that _____

_____

I would be confident of having successfully overcome

this ostrich problem if _____

How hard was that to fill out? Not so difficult that it put you off, I hope, but difficult enough to make you stop and think. A problem that is too easy to describe may not be the one that is the most important for you to tackle. Okay. You've got a defined problem, you know what fear may be causing it, and you've gotten a good idea as to how you would feel or what might happen if your ostrich were out of your life.

The Ostrich Goal Statement is little more than setting your goal down in black and white. Your statement protects you from the ostrich's wiliest ways because nothing can change the words you've written on this piece of paper. Read aloud what you've written. How does it feel to hear it spoken in addition to seeing it in writing? Isn't it good to get it out in the open?

Once you do feel good about your Goal Statement, you are ready to select the change techniques that can help you reach your goal and are suited to your personality. Since we want to use your personality information in choosing the "best" techniques, copy your personality profile from page 119 to a similar graph I've placed on page 202.

Regardless of how you scored on the two scales, you ended up as one of the four types (unless you scored "8" on both scales). There are, of course, an infinite number of subtle variations within each of the types. You'll find, however, that a rough description of which change techniques are most appropriate for personality and ostrich styles in each personality type can help you zero in on the techniques that are right for you. Let's look at each of the quadrants and match techniques to style.

Type I-A Internal/Aggressive: "*I'll* do it—or else!"
Someone with this personality style tends to be aggressive and to view life from the perspective of an internal locus of control. For you this means that an ostrich is very likely to set you at odds with a threatening and powerful source of problems from outside. Your ostrich takes advantage of your high sense of responsibility and your aggressive outward style. You may react to situations with hostility even when they aren't threatening, particularly when things aren't perfect. Perfectionism is one of this quadrant's likely ostrich behaviors.

The most widely used technique for dealing with perfectionism as an ostrich behavior is the *Persian rug ploy,* or planned imperfection. Most of us who have gotten deeply

INTERNAL LOCUS OF CONTROL

	16	
	15	
	14	
Type I-P	13	**Type I-A**
Personality	12	**Personality**
	11	
	10	
	9	

PASSIVE 0--1--2--3--4--5--6--7--8 --9--10--11--12--13--14--15--16 **AGGRESSIVE**

	7	
Type E-P	6	**Type E-A**
	5	
Personality	4	**Personality**
	3	
	2	
	1	
	0	

EXTERNAL LOCUS OF CONTROL

involved in a project, whether in art, architecture, furniture arrangement, or even writing a book, have suffered from the intrusion of this ostrich. The project nears its assigned deadline, and, for some reason, we still stubbornly review each detail, going over everything "one last time." But, of course, it isn't the last time, because we will go over it again and again. At some point, the more time we spend on it, the less we get done, and the project invariably suffers—not from any major flaw, but from delay.

Using the Persian rug ploy can offset the high need to be in control. You may produce a project that is actually more complete than if you were to go over and over it, looking for that one last "typo." By planning and accepting a flaw that is not crucial or damaging to the whole, you are in a very real way warning yourself to create the distance necessary for some perspective on the task. This ploy brings with it an element of humor that can defuse potentially hot confrontations, because you are, in a sense, sabotaging the work in some purposeful yet trivial way.

People with high internal locus of control like *to appear* in control even when they feel that they really aren't. For Walter such an *appearance* of control was important. Walter had to learn to be comfortable with the idea of *advertising* a lapse in his control. The mere thought of losing control can generate high anxiety and, of course, please the ostrich. With *guided imagery* and *self-rehearsal*, as well as some *role-playing* of specific situations, Walter was able to show others his concerns about losing control.

Internal/aggressive people almost always have an Ostrich Complex that takes a heavy toll on their control over time. For you, *time management* techniques, particularly *delegating* and *dumping*, are excellent starting places for regaining real control of your time each day. *Action lists* can also play an important role here.

It's likely that just when you thought you were making progress, the ostrich will bring you face to face with a powerful someone who takes control and makes you *angry*. Don't be fooled by the temptation to "let that person have it" under the guise of being *assertive*. If you are angry and feel the need to express it, it's important for you to gain control and plan how and when you will express that anger. Never do so spontaneously in the situation that the ostrich tells you has actually provoked your anger. Study the steps for expressing anger and being assertive. Learn the differences and use the techniques associated with each to your benefit.

The *double-duty letter* and *planned stress* are also appropriate techniques for internal/aggressive individuals who want to oust their ostriches. These techniques are good ways to rechannel that anger, which might otherwise become so damaging. Managers who have caught the ostrich setting up a home in their departments should provide opportunities—specially scheduled ones at that—for their employees to use for releasing some of the natural frustration that builds up in all work settings. Some managers schedule an early morning "open door" time, either by appointment or on a drop-in basis, for employees who want to sit over coffee and chat. Others use small group discussions each month, similar to a politician's town forum meeting. These and similar opportunities can relieve tensions and thus make those tensions less threatening.

Personality Type E-A External/Aggressive: "*I* want *you* to do it—or else!" The more extreme your scores, the more helpless you feel about being able to change things—and the angrier you are about being this way.

Since you view "the situation" as so important in running your life, you need to find out how that situation can be made to work for you. One way to accomplish an ostrich-free state is to manage the situation so that it will take care of you the way you want it to. We've all seen secretaries who are in control of the boss, and we hear example after example of people who admit to being controlled by someone who works below them. Managing the boss is a time-honored practice that is often the most harmonious accommodation available.

The external/aggressive ostrich needs to be handled with techniques such as those that deal with *interruptions*: Close the door to your work space; put up a "Beware" sign; use your answering machine. Use the *ostrich box* and *ostrich memo* liberally to help you focus on where the control really is.

Deirdre is aggressive yet she had a strong sense that control over her life lies outside herself. I had Deirdre draw up some very simple schedules that had nothing to do with the legal cases that she listed on her goal statement. We did this so that she could get used to the process of scheduling and taking control over some of her activities. We then proceeded, always according to her schedule, to work with other techniques and apply them to her goal statement.

We then began to work *on her work* by having her make lists relevant to her cases, assign priorities, and discard unimportant items. Since fretting and fumbling had become part of Deirdre's ostrich style, you'll remember that I also had her schedule some *stew time*. We even planned the *trivia* that she could stew over.

Type E-P External/Passive: "*You* decide; I don't care."
People who have an external locus of control perspective
and feel passive need to be sure that the source of their
outside control points them in the direction they want to
go. External/passive ostriches thrive on collecting and
other passive ways of dealing with anger, frustration, and
fears. These other passive ways include exaggerated compliance or extreme subservience to the perception of someone else's power. In situations where a person feels humili-
ated and life seems hopeless, this type of compliance
actually increases the power of the opponent. Such behavior in a TV sit-com usually inspires laughter. In real life it
is among the most pathetic of all reactions to stress.

One of the most significant change techniques for an
ostrich with this personality style is the *self-agenda* (page
188). This involves drawing up a specific statement of
your goals and requirements for a particular discussion or
negotiation. It can take the form of a simple list of needs,
or include a plan of action for expressing those needs. It
can be a combination flow chart and meeting schedule,
such as the one I had Glenn construct *before* he went in to
see Mr. Stevens. Here's what one of his practice self-
agendas looked like. He went through four of them before
he felt good about one that really seemed like his.

Self-Agenda for Meeting with Mr. Stevens

A. My Needs:
   1. Clear priorities for tasks.
   2. A specifically limited number of tasks—not neces-
      sarily few, but *defined*.

3. Clear deadlines—so that tasks won't be due before a previously agreed-upon date or time.

B. Stevens' Needs:
1. To look good.
2. To get the work done that he's been assigned to do.
3. To be seen as effective by upper management.
4. To be able to get things done on short notice.
5. To be considered a strong and supported manager.

C. Subject of Meeting (unstated by Stevens—I should ask for clear advance notice of his agenda so I can prepare):
1. Stevens will probably have another task to assign. If he does, discuss its priority right away. Try to go on to discussing my need for regular meetings about the priority of all tasks.
2. Stevens may want meeting to complain about divisional reorganization. Again, bring up need to know priorities, as well as advance notice so I can prepare. Let him know I can be more supportive if he gives me such notice.
3. Bring up his need to be responsive to upstairs. Make sure to express it as *our* need. Suggest that it can be done by limiting the number of tasks and having clear deadlines—so that extra or emergency tasks can be slotted into the schedule without throwing everything out of whack. Tell him about triage technique problems.
4. Don't murder Stevens and don't quit if none of this happens as I plan.

By developing agendas similar to this one before each contact with Mr. Stevens, sometimes as hastily as during the two minutes he had between the meeting notice and the time he left his office, Glenn was able to express his personal needs to his boss. An important point is that he was able to express what he wanted and needed in the context of what Stevens wanted and needed as well.

As you can imagine, it never went just as Glenn had planned or hoped, but we had role-played such possibilities so that intense frustration never developed. But the meetings followed Glenn's scenarios often enough that he was gradually able to get Stevens to recognize and meet many of Glenn's own needs. An important moment in their relationship came when Glenn realized that Stevens had never been aware of the stress his behavior had produced in Glenn. This mutual discovery served to reward both Glenn for taking the risk and his boss for being willing to be open enough to hear him out. They, and their company, benefited from their new form of communication and awareness.

If you are the external/passive personality type, you already know that you tend to be passive. I'll wager that people (your friends mostly) have tried to get you to act more aggressively to reach your goals. I'll also bet that it hasn't worked; and that, in fact, whenever you've tried aggression it misfired and you went away confirming to yourself that you'll never make it. That's what happened with Gary. Has the same thing ever happened for you?

It is important for people who drift toward the passive end of the scale to function assertively at times; but as you saw in the techniques section, being assertive does not mean being aggressive. Glenn let his *self-agenda* guide him through the three steps of the *assertive* process: How I feel; What has happened; What can we do about it? Glenn also used *logical negotiation* to help him get what he was after.

Logical negotiation was used to keep Stevens' attention focused on how his own needs would be met, even enhanced, if he followed Glenn's suggestions. Instead of banging on the table and shouting, or even showing Stevens up in some sort of competitive game, Glenn made sure that his requests were phrased so they also allowed Stevens to look good. This method is akin to using the carrot instead of the stick. Since Glenn is Stevens' subordinate, he has little in the way of a stick to use, and he must recognize that. The techniques he used let him take the lead in the situation while Stevens clearly remained the boss. In a sense Glenn also used a form of *guided imagery* and projected it so that his boss could appreciate the positive scenario he was envisioning and see the roles that both might have in making something positive happen. In addition, *role-playing* and *self-rehearsal* were also important to Glenn when he was preparing to discuss his issues with Stevens. When there is a need to meet with and deal with an aggressive person, these techniques should be used to rehearse the meeting. The result will be a lower level of anxiety and less likelihood that the Ostrich Complex will take over.

Identify any task that requires you to act assertively and treat it as a *distasteful task*. It should be done first, keeping in mind the three steps that are essential to effective assertiveness. The *ostrich box* and *ostrich memo* will also help you handle such distasteful tasks more effectively.

Here's a warning. Watch out that you don't become

perfectionistic as you implement these techniques. For example, the ostrich can have you revising your *self-agenda* forever—or for so long that you never get to act on it. Glenn was in danger of falling into a perfectionistic style as he moved from draft to draft. We dealt with that problem by working up an intentionally sloppy draft that still had all the necessary components. Glenn agreed to go right from that one to the final one, regardless of how imperfectly it turned out. Remember, enough is enough. Know when to recognize you have reached the point of diminishing returns, and you'll gain that extra needed bit of control.

Type I-P Internal/Passive: "I want to do it; but I don't mind if you do it." If you score here, you like to think that events are under your control, but you often don't bother to take effective action to control them. This means that you feel super-responsible for following through on frameworks you've been handed by others. They then become "yours." When things then do go wrong, you develop anxiety about the problems and then fret about your worrying.

Use *break the loop* (page 171) to break into this cycle of self-perpetuating ostrich-induced anxiety. Practice *guided imagery* first and then bring in *self-rehearsal* to help you see the paths available to you as possible solutions. With an internal/passive style, you can effectively solve the problem in your mind and then have difficulty putting your plan into action. Procrastination is the danger behavior here. Your new behaviors must be performed externally, not just in your mind, so let *self-rehearsal* help you move from mental to real-life actions. You can then move on to *role-playing* to get a true feel for the changes you want to put into place.

Be sure that you provide *success experiences* for yourself at every step of every stage. Plan them, don't just hope they occur. Think of yourself as needing to be refueled along a journey in the same way that you refuel your car on a trip. That's what *success experiences* are for—to give you that energy to make it to the next stop.

One of your tasks is to make your passivity a voluntary activity rather than an automatic response to stress. Turn passivity into something you can choose to do (or not do) by practicing it on purpose in inappropriate situations. It's a type of *Persian rug ploy,* isn't it? This lets a passive response become in reality an active response, one that's under your control. *Advertise* your passivity as you get used to controlling it in certain situations: "I can't decide what movie to see. I'm too passive a person. You decide."

Margaret used most of the techniques I've discussed for the external/passive personality type. She still prefers to avoid any type of confrontation, but now she realizes that this is the part of her personality most open to the live-in ostrich.

The Multi-Type Ostrich. You may wonder why snippets of techniques for personality types other than yours still sound good for your ostrich. Remember that an ostrich can live in more than one part of your life. The way in which you use aspects of your personality style may vary from work to home to interpersonal relationships depending on the demands and your fears. At work you may be internal/aggressive and yet become external/passive in certain interpersonal relationships. Remember Roy? There's an example of how normal it is to develop different behavior patterns in different situations or life spheres. Patterns can change as you change the context in which you're functioning. That's why it was so important for you to examine where your ostrich lived, as you did in Chapter Four. Very few people are only one personality type across all areas of their lives. But you can use the prescriptions for each type to go after the ostrich that has moved into a specific area for you, and then change techniques as you change problems.

A Generic Prescription, After All. I do have a few points that should be remembered and applied by anyone embarking on a change program. They relate to the general behavior change ideas I listed at the beginning of Chapter Nine.

If you are going it alone, using this book as your guide, remember how important it is to *divide and conquer*. The bigger the problem, the more components it has. Tackle problems in clearly limited stages. Don't try to do too much at once—that tactic is your ostrich's way of stopping you in your hunt. Tackling too large a problem can lead to exhaustion and to frustration with this program and, more important, with yourself. Your goal is not to change *you*; your goal is to change your *behavior*.

Another key to all of these techniques is the concrete definition of your goals. We have defined goals at several stages in this program, but can you remember yours right now? If not, look back at what they are. Keep them in mind no matter which part you're reading. Use them as your map, showing you where you were and the route to where you want to be. If you are not sure of where you're headed, it will be difficult for you to know how successful you have been—and will be.

New! New! New! Every personal Ostrich Complex you identify will seem like a brand-new one. This means that it's not very effective to apply the same techniques to each ostrich you've located. Each has to be understood and changed on its own merits. You become susceptible to another ostrich when you become too mechanical in handling what happens in your life, when you assume that all problems can be treated in the same way. Staying ostrich-free is a lot like keeping physically fit—you need to watch what you let into your system, and you need to give your positive behavior patterns plenty of exercise.

As you practice your choice of techniques, you'll find some very similar to hard work. They are. But the gains can be wonderful. Freeing yourself from the Ostrich Complex takes a lot of real work to make your changes work. You've done a lot already. And you know that you have all the equipment you need to finish the job. Are you going to do it? Great!

TYPES AND TECHNIQUES
AT A GLANCE

Some behavior-change techniques lend themselves particularly well for use with one or more of the personality types we've discussed. I've listed many of the techniques below with an accompanying list of the personality types for which each works well. Read through them to see which apply best to your particular personality type, but do consider all of the behavior-change techniques, however, as you design your own prescription for freeing yourself of the Ostrich Complex.

Behavior Change Technique	Particularly Useful for These Personality Types			
	I-A	E-A	E-P	I-P
Action Lists		x	x	
Advertising	x			x
Anger: Dealing with	x	x		
Assertiveness Steps	x		x	
Behavior Modification	x	x	x	x
Breaking the Loop				x
Distancing	x	x		
Distasteful Tasks			x	
Divide and Conquer	x	x	x	x
Double-Duty Letter	x	x	x	x
Guided Imagery	x	x	x	x
"I" Statements		x	x	
Interruptions		x	x	
Logical Negotiation			x	
Moving Away	x			x
Ostrich Box		x	x	
Ostrich Memo		x	x	
Persian Rug Ploy	x			x
Planned Stress	x	x		
Role-Playing	x		x	x
Schedules		x		
Scheduling Recreation	x	x		
Self-Agenda			x	
Self-Rehearsal	x		x	x
Stew Time	x	x		
Success Experiences			x	x
Time Management	x	x	x	x
Triage		x	x	

Chapter 11

Saying Goodbye: Closing the Door to Your Ostrich Complex

It's time to say goodbye to your Ostrich Complex—and goodbye to the problems that ostriching has caused you.

You know what the Ostrich Complex looks like; you know what ostriching can do. But you've also learned how to deal with ostriched problems when they appear. Most important, perhaps, you've learned a lot about who you are and how to express yourself. Most people never get as far as you have. Their ostriching keeps them in the dark.

You've also learned how hard it is to change some habits. If your ostrich has been around for a while, it was probably pretty well dug in. I know how hard it has been for me with some particularly ornery behavior patterns I've established. I've changed some—and I've failed with some others.

It takes courage to tackle an ostrich that's been dug in. But those of us who have tried to change know one thing that others don't. It's that no matter how difficult change may seem, it is possible. After getting this far in dealing with your Ostrich Complex, I'm sure you know that. Give yourself credit for your effort, even if success wasn't all that you hoped it would be yet. You deserve credit for the effort you've made and for what you have been able to learn and do.

Forewarned is Forearmed: The Ostrich Gambit. There is, though, one crucial warning that I want to share with you. It is the last thing that I learned from tackling my own ostrich problems, and it has come up for everyone with whom I've ever worked.

Let's assume you have managed to free yourself; you've gotten rid of a problem that had been making you miserable, reducing your happiness and interfering with reaching your life's goals. Great! Congratulations! And look out! You are vulnerable to the most subtle aspect of the Ostrich Complex—the *Ostrich Gambit*.

The Ostrich Gambit is a desperate attempt by your exposed-to-the-light ostrich to bury its head and your problem once again. Here's how it works. When we accomplish something worthwhile, such as getting rid of an ostrich, establishing a healthy relationship with someone we love, or becoming head of our company, we relax. After all, we've won the fight or achieved what we hoped so we tell ourselves we deserve a break. At that very moment we risk becoming sloppy. We stop watching for the danger signals. We forget what professional athletes have known for years, that coasting after a victory is an invitation to disaster.

As you get sloppy in dealing with other people and everyday problems, the ostrich digs its way back into your life. No matter how hard you've worked and how far you've come in dealing with your Ostrich Complex, keep in mind that *you cannot allow yourself to get sloppy.* Like an Olympic medal winner, you must keep working out to stay in shape, even though you may never have to compete again. And you must stay attuned to the attitudes and behaviors of those around you, for they may change, even if you don't. Those changes may provide an opening for the ostrich to move back into your life.

"Enough is enough," you may say. "When do I finally get it right and keep my ostrich away for good?"

You will—sooner or later—but it takes time for the new ways you have developed to respond to your ostrich and to old anxiety and fears to become permanent. It takes time for you to learn that you no longer need to procrastinate or deny or collect or be perfect when faced with those old stress situations.

But the ostrich is like an epidemic disease. Long after an effective treatment has been developed and given to most of the world's population, the disease will surface unexpectedly. This happens because the organism causing the disease has mutated sufficiently to resist the old effective treatment. The treatment must then be modified to deal with the new strain. So it is when the ostrich reappears, in a modified form, as an unsatisfactory response to a new problem.

You've done well and there's no doubt that you can be ready for any future ostrich problems if you are prepared.

You know the techniques to use when you feel the ostrich moving into your life. It's important now to be able to see the Ostrich Gambit taking place and gauge the potential for the return of the ostrich into your life.

The Ostrich Early Warning System. In order for you to be aware of the ostrich and its gambit, I'm going to provide you with a checklist I've found helpful. I call it my Ostrich Early Warning System. It has two aspects; two kinds of items. One type consists of typical behaviors that warn of the ostrich's approach. The other type contains the kinds of things that we say to ourselves under the early influence of the ostrich.

Remember that this is my personal checklist. Some of the items are generally applicable to everyone; but some only fit my *personal* ostrich, or an ostrich who has lived with one of my clients. I am sharing my checklist with you so that you can design *your* own personal Ostrich Early Warning System.

The checklist doesn't get scored or transferred into quadrants. On the contrary, it's really easy to use and to design. You can go through it in just a few minutes every month or so, just to make sure that the Ostrich Gambit isn't operating in your life. Just check the items that apply to you, and leave the rest blank. Then go back and try to detect any pattern that exists among the items that you've checked. Another checklist is in the Appendix for you to copy and use in the future in case you find my items helpful.

THE OSTRICH EARLY WARNING SYSTEM CHECKLIST

_____ **1.** My Action Lists often contain the same item(s) each time I rewrite them.

_____ **2.** I've been going out of my way to avoid someone with whom I really should be dealing.

_____ **3.** I've been watching more TV than usual, without choosing specific programs.

_____ **4.** I'm sleeping more than I used to but I don't feel well rested.

_____ **5.** Someone I know and see frequently has started talking about being bothered by something I consider to be insignificant.

_____ **6.** My work has been piling up, but I know I'll get to it soon.

_____ **7.** I need to know a lot more about an important project I've got to do before I can really get started on it.

_____ **8.** The little details in a present project seem to be taking longer than I thought to work out so I can't wrap up the project.

_____ **9.** I worry more about details than I used to.

_____ **10.** I could finish my present project if I had a better idea of how well I'm doing.

_____ 11. That's the last time I'm going to put up with _____'s behavior!

_____ 12. I didn't need that (raise; person; job; prize; ____) anyway.

_____ 13. I'd like to change my career track, but I can't figure out what would be better.

_____ 14. Most of the people around me seem to have more fun than I do.

_____ 15. If I only had a different (job relationship; place to live; _____), I'd be much happier.

_____ 16. _____ is holding me back from reaching my goals.

_____ 17. Nobody ever comes through for me when I need something.

_____ 18. Whenever I talk with _____, I find myself changing the subject frequently.

_____ 19. The more effort I put into _____ (name the task), the worse it gets.

_____ 20. I'm just not cut out to be (loved; successful; ____).

_____ 21. I've recently lost my temper more than I used to.

_____ 22. If it doesn't happen the way I want it to, I'll just keep quiet about it.

_____ **23.** I'm assigned all the menial tasks. Nobody gives me anything really important to do.

_____ **24.** I'm the only one who can do things right around here.

_____ **25.** It's easier to do something important for someone else than it is to do the same thing for myself.

_____ **26.** I've been planning to _____, and I will, as soon as I can.

_____ **27.** There's always an emergency that comes up at work to keep me from getting things done.

_____ **28.** I'd rather not think about _____ too much; it makes me nervous.

_____ **29.** Many times I just don't know what to say or how to say it.

_____ **30.** I have more trouble than I used to saying what I want to say at meetings.

_____ **31.** I can't seem to stop worrying/daydreaming about _____.

_____ **32.** There's so much I have to do that I can't figure out where to start.

_____ **33.** The more I think about _____, the more confusing it gets.

_____ **34.** I have trouble deciding which tasks are the most important.

_____ **35.** I've been doing a lot of "busywork" like cleaning, organizing, and the like around deadline time.

_____ **36.** I'll get to it as soon as _____ happens.

_____ **37.** If only I could get the right idea for _____, I'd have it made.

_____ **38.** _____ seems to be the one person blocking my chances for getting ahead.

_____ **39.** If _____ does that to me one more time, I'll go talk to our superiors about it.

_____ **40.** If I say something about it, I'll be blamed for everything that goes wrong.

_____ **41.** It's a fine idea but our employees could not adapt to it.

_____ **42.** We don't do that here.

_____ **43.** In a hundred years, who's going to care?

That's my checklist. Use it as a model. I know you can come up with something similar—but designed just for you. You know _your_ Ostrich Complex, and you have the results of your tests and work from the previous chapters to draw from.

Once you've created your personalized Ostrich Early Warning Checklist, post it somewhere convenient. Consult it often and compare the items you check one month with those you checked the month before. Your checklist can warn you of things you might not notice if the Ostrich Complex Gambit is beginning to move in on you. My advice is to use it for the next six months, and consult earlier chapters as you feel the need arise.

When to Bring in the Pro. We've talked about what the Ostrich Complex is, what it can do to you, and what you can do about it. Many of the people you've met thus far handled theirs with a written program similar to the one you've been using. Others dug through their problems in my office, one week at a time. Seeing a professional therapist or counselor can be a practical alternative to dealing with your ostrich by yourself. Is it a good idea for you?

You've worked through this book; take a look at your results—or lack of results. If the work you've done has clarified problems and has or will facilitate positive change, then you are in an excellent position to continue by yourself. If, however, things have gotten murky, and no clear problems to work on have separated themselves from your feelings of general confusion, then professional help is the best way to proceed. If you suspect that an Ostrich Complex has gotten you so far down that you don't feel you can dig your own way out, then that help is just what the doctor has ordered. Find a therapist who will help you address the *specific problems* you're experiencing. And do it soon.

Because some types of therapy breed even more ostrich problems, find a therapist whose personality and style say, ''Let's look at what's bothering you and plan some strategies for change.'' The ostrich loves therapy that says, instead, "Let's probe around for a year or two before we confront anything." You have to confront the ostrich, at some point, if you want it out of your life. It may take some time for you and your therapist to decide on the best time for that confrontation and on the best techniques for you, *personally*. But don't wait or let your therapist wait too long. If you do, the very problem you need to deal with will keep you from ever dealing with your problems. So the next question is: When?

The Best Time Is . . . When? The best time to deal with your Ostrich Complex, of course, is now. But that's not the only time. You now know that you have to deal with it sometime. That time has to feel right to you. It has to be a time when the energy and motivation to change are there for you. The important thing, whether you decide to deal with your ostrich now or later, is that you are deciding to deal with it.

Remember that the Ostrich Complex works by causing paralysis. It blocks your ability to decide. If you evade making a decision one way or the other, you've given your ostrich a firmer hold on your life. It's going to be that much harder to yank it out when you do finally decide to take action. On the other hand, if you actually decide to do *nothing* at present, you've still moved your ostrich a little more into the light—you are still making a decision.

The Best Technique . . . Nothing? One of my friends has developed "doing nothing" to a state of fine art. She imagines it quite concretely as taking a problem and putting it away in a box until she feels ready to deal with it. She knows what the problem is, what its costs are, and has a good sense of her own strengths and weaknesses, yet she chooses to put the problem into the box. The box is clearly labeled and she reviews it once in a while and makes a new "to deal with it or not" decision. What she does *not* do is constantly fret and worry over it. Instead, she makes very definite choices as part of a regular review process.

In other words, she *regains control* by doing what might be an ostrich behavior if she had drifted into it unwittingly. Her control consists of the reverse—not drifting into ostriching unwillingly or unknowingly, but choosing voluntarily, deliberately, and joyfully to delay acting.

Not doing anything about your Ostrich Complex can actually be among the strongest anti-ostrich techniques at your disposal.

Looking Into the Future: I See . . . Using any approach we've discussed doesn't mean that all of your ostrich problems will vanish instantly. In fact, the truth is far from it. It does mean, however, that you have regained control over your power of decision, and that means that you have a foothold in your own life again.

You're close to finishing this book. I hope that our time together won't end with this chapter, though. Instead, I want you occasionally to turn to earlier pages and read them again with the new insights you have gained. You now know your ostrich and your ostrich tendencies intimately. And you're well on your way to regaining a feeling of control over what happens to you and how you can effectively deal with it. No longer do you feel like a leaf blown about in the wind. I hope you feel that you are now the doer rather than the person to whom things are done.

Isn't that why you were interested in this topic and in how to deal with your ostrich problems?

You will close this book, but keep it—and its ideas—around for a while. Look over your worksheets in a month and then in another month. Check the danger signals you find occurring at work, at home, and in your interpersonal relationships. Examine the effects that a lingering or returning ostrich behavior may be having on your life. Evaluate what you are doing to change those effects and fend off any returning ostrich.

Whenever you need it, take a quick refresher course by skimming Chapter Four and Chapter Nine. They may be all you need.

And remember, even after all this, if you decide to do nothing now, at least you know that the groundwork has been laid. You are well prepared for dealing with your ostrich in the future. Success will be just a matter of going through with it; you already know what to do.

Look how far you've come. And at what you've gained. Here's proof of your success, your Ostrich Certificate. Unlike most awards, however, this one you award to yourself for the work you've done. After all, who else deserves to award it to you? Who else knows where you started and how far you've come? Congratulations!

THE OSTRICH COMPLEX
DIPLOMA

★

This is to certify that _____
has successfully pulled his/her head out of
the sand and graduated from THE OSTRICH
COMPLEX. The graduate is now entitled to
all the business and personal effectiveness
and happiness accorded thereto.

Dated this _____ day of _____, 19___

_____
Elliot Weiner, Ph.D.
Instructor

OSTRICHUS RESTARE UN PAX

Notes

1. Kenneth Pelletier, *Healthy People in Unhealthy Places: Stress and Fitness at Work* (New York: Delacorte Press, 1984), p. 59.

2. P. Dworkin, "Job Stress Claims on the Increase," *San Francisco Chronicle*, March 1, 1985, p. 2.

3. Daniel Goleman, *Vital Lies, Simple Truths: The Psychology of Self-deception and Shared Illusions* (New York: Simon & Schuster, 1985).

4. Connell Cowan and Melvyn Kinder, *Smart Women, Foolish Choices* (New York: Clarkson Potter, 1985).

5. Metropolitan Life Association, *National Newspaper*

Advertisement (New York: Metropolitan Life Insurance Company, 1982).

6. Accountemps, Inc. "Survey of Personnel Executives at 100 Large Companies," *USA Today*, March 29, 1985.

7. Lee Iacocca, *Iacocca: An Autobiography* (New York: Bantam, 1984), p. 112.

8. Perry London and Charles Spielberger, "Job Stress, Hassles, and Medical Risk," *American Health*, March/April, 1983, p. 114.

9. London and Spielberger, p. 114.

10. Harry Levinson, "Coping with 'Fear, Anxiety,' of a Corporate Merger" *U.S. News and World Report*, September 24, 1984.

11. Ibid.

12. Paul Watzlawick, John Weakland, and Richard Fisch, *Change* (New York: W.W. Norton, 1974), p. 110.

13. Albert Ellis and R. A. Harper, *A New Guide to Rational Living* (North Hollywood, CA: Wilshire Book Co., 1975).

14. "Wall Street Journal Report," USA Cable Television Network, May 28, 1985.

Suggested Reading

Alberti, Robert, and Michael Emmons. *Your Perfect Right: A Guide to Assertive Behavior*. San Luis Obispo, CA: Impact, 1974.

Burka, Jane, and Lenora Yuen. *Procrastination: Why You Do It, What to Do About It*. New York: Addison-Wesley, 1983.

Burns, David. *Feeling Good: The New Mood Therapy*. New York: William Morrow, 1980.

Freudenberger, Herbert, and Gail North. *Situational Anxiety: How to Overcome Your Everyday Anxious Moments*. New York: Anchor Press, 1982.

Lakein, Alan. *How to Get Control of Your Time and Your Life*. New York: Peter Wyden, 1973.

Pelletier, Kenneth. *Mind As Healer, Mind As Slayer: A Holistic Approach to Preventing Stress Disorders*. New York: Delacorte and Delta, 1977.

Rubin, Theodore Isaac. *The Angry Book*. New York: Collier Books, 1969.

Selye, Hans. *Stress Without Distress*. New York: Signet, 1974.

Warren, Neil Clark. *Make Anger Your Ally*. New York: Doubleday, 1983.

Weisinger, Hendrie, and Norman Lobsenz. *Nobody's Perfect: How to Give Criticism and Get Results*. New York: Warner Books, 1981.

Ziglar, Zig. *Steps to the Top*. Gretna, LA: Pelican, 1985.

Appendix

THE OSTRICH COMPLEX INVENTORY

ANSWER SHEET

Totally Unlike Me	Very Little Like Me	Equally Like And Unlike Me	Very Much Like Me	Totally Like Me
1	2	3	4	5

Answer each of the questions by selecting the appropriate number from the scale above and writing that number below. Some of the questions will be more difficult to answer than others but answer each one as best you can. After you've answered all forty questions, turn to page 63 for directions on how to score your Ostrich Complex Inventory.

Perfectionism	Denial	Collecting	Procrastination
1. _____	2. _____	3. _____	4. _____
5. _____	6. _][_ *	7. _][_ *	8. _____
9. _____	10._____	11._____	12._____
13._][_ *	14._____	15._____	16._____
17._____	18._____	19._____	20._][_ *
21._][_ *	22._____	23._____	24._____
25._____	26._][_ *	27._][_ *	28._____
29._][_ *	30._][_ *	31._____	32._____
33._][_ *	34._____	35._][_ *	36._____
37._____	38._____	39._____	40._][_ *

[   ] + [   ] + [   ] + [   ] = _____
   1   2   3   4   OQ

THE OSTRICH COMPLEX INVENTORY

ANSWER SHEET

Totally Unlike Me	Very Little Like Me	Equally Like And Unlike Me	Very Much Like Me	Totally Like Me
1	2	3	4	5

Answer each of the questions by selecting the appropriate number from the scale above and writing that number below. Some of the questions will be more difficult to answer than others but answer each one as best you can. After you've answered all forty questions, turn to page 63 for directions on how to score your Ostrich Complex Inventory.

Perfectionism	Denial	Collecting	Procrastination
1. _____	2. _____	3. _____	4. _____
5. _____	6. _]\[_*	7. _]\[_*	8. _____
9. _____	10._____	11._____	12._____
13._]\[_*	14._____	15._____	16._____
17._____	18._____	19._____	20._]\[_*
21._]\[_*	22._____	23._____	24._____
25._____	26._]\[_*	27._]\[_*	28._____
29._]\[_*	30._]\[_*	31._____	32._____
33._]\[_*	34._____	35._]\[_*	36._____
37._____	38._____	39._____	40._]\[_*

[   ] + [   ] + [   ] + [   ] = _____
   1   2   3   4   OQ

THE OSTRICH COMPLEX INVENTORY

ANSWER SHEET

Totally	*Very Little*	*Equally Like*	*Very Much*	*Totally*
Unlike Me	*Like Me*	*And Unlike Me*	*Like Me*	*Like Me*
1	2	3	4	5

Answer each of the questions by selecting the appropriate number from the scale above and writing that number below. Some of the questions will be more difficult to answer than others but answer each one as best you can. After you've answered all forty questions, turn to page 63 for directions on how to score your Ostrich Complex Inventory.

Perfectionism	*Denial*	*Collecting*	*Procrastination*
1. _____	2. _____	3. _____	4. _____
5. _____	6. _][_ *	7. _][_ *	8. _____
9. _____	10._____	11._____	12._____
13._][_ *	14._____	15._____	16._____
17._____	18._____	19._____	20._][_ *
21._][_ *	22._____	23._____	24._____
25._____	26._][_ *	27._][_ *	28._____
29._][_ *	30._][_ *	31._____	32._____
33._][_ *	34._____	35._][_ *	36._____
37._____	38._____	39._____	40._][_ *

[   ]   +   [   ]   +   [   ]   +   [   ]   =   _____

  1   2   3   4   OQ

THE OSTRICH EARLY WARNING SYSTEM CHECKLIST

_____ 1. My Action Lists often contain the same item(s) each time I rewrite them.

_____ 2. I've been going out of my way to avoid someone with whom I really should be dealing.

_____ 3. I've been watching more TV than usual, without choosing specific programs.

_____ 4. I'm sleeping more than I used to but I don't feel well rested.

_____ 5. Someone I know and see frequently has started talking about being bothered by something I consider to be insignificant.

_____ 6. My work has been piling up, but I know I'll get to it soon.

_____ 7. I need to know a lot more about an important project I've got to do before I can really get started on it.

_____ 8. The little details in a present project seem to be taking longer than I thought to work out so I can't wrap up the project.

_____ 9. I worry more about details than I used to.

_____ 10. I could finish my present project if I had a better idea of how well I'm doing.

_____ **11.** That's the last time I'm going to put up with _____'s behavior!

_____ **12.** I didn't need that (raise; person; job; prize; ____) anyway.

_____ **13.** I'd like to change my career track, but I can't figure out what would be better.

_____ **14.** Most of the people around me seem to have more fun than I do.

_____ **15.** If I only had a different (job relationship; place to live; _____), I'd be much happier.

_____ **16.** _____ is holding me back from reaching my goals.

_____ **17.** Nobody ever comes through for me when I need something.

_____ **18.** Whenever I talk with _____, I find myself changing the subject frequently.

_____ **19.** The more effort I put into _____ (name the task), the worse it gets.

_____ **20.** I'm just not cut out to be (loved; successful; ____).

_____ **21.** I've recently lost my temper more than I used to.

_____ **22.** If it doesn't happen the way I want it to, I'll just keep quiet about it.

_____ 23. I'm assigned all the menial tasks. Nobody gives me anything really important to do.

_____ 24. I'm the only one who can do things right around here.

_____ 25. It's easier to do something important for someone else than it is to do the same thing for myself.

_____ 26. I've been planning to _____, and I will, as soon as I can.

_____ 27. There's always an emergency that comes up at work to keep me from getting things done.

_____ 28. I'd rather not think about _____ too much; it makes me nervous.

_____ 29. Many times I just don't know what to say or how to say it.

_____ 30. I have more trouble than I used to saying what I want to say at meetings.

_____ 31. I can't seem to stop worrying/daydreaming about _____.

_____ 32. There's so much I have to do that I can't figure out where to start.

_____ 33. The more I think about _____, the more confusing it gets.

_____ 34. I have trouble deciding which tasks are the most important.

_____ **35.** I've been doing a lot of "busywork" like cleaning, organizing, and the like around deadline time.

_____ **36.** I'll get to it as soon as _____ happens.

_____ **37.** If only I could get the right idea for _____, I'd have it made.

_____ **38.** _____ seems to be the one person blocking my chances for getting ahead.

_____ **39.** If _____ does that to me one more time, I'll go talk to our superiors about it.

_____ **40.** If I say something about it, I'll be blamed for everything that goes wrong.

_____ **41.** It's a fine idea but our employees could not adapt to it.

_____ **42.** We don't do that here.

_____ **43.** In a hundred years, who's going to care?

By the year 2000, 2 out of 3 Americans could be illiterate.

It's true.

Today, 75 million adults... about one American in three, can't read adequately. And by the year 2000, U.S. News & World Report envisions an America with a literacy rate of only 30%.

Before that America comes to be, you can stop it... by joining the fight against illiteracy today.

Call the Coalition for Literacy at toll-free **1-800-228-8813** and volunteer.

Volunteer Against Illiteracy. The only degree you need is a degree of caring.

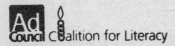

Ad Council Coalition for Literacy

Warner Books is proud to be an active supporter of the Coalition for Literacy.